T0323596

Cambridge Elements ≡

Elements in Ancient and Pre-modern Economies
edited by
Kenneth G. Hirth
The Pennsylvania State University
Timothy Earle
Northwestern University
Emily J. Kate
The University of Vienna

ANCIENT MAYA ECONOMIES

Scott R. Hutson
University of Kentucky

CAMBRIDGE
UNIVERSITY PRESS

Shaftesbury Road, Cambridge CB2 8EA, United Kingdom

One Liberty Plaza, 20th Floor, New York, NY 10006, USA

477 Williamstown Road, Port Melbourne, VIC 3207, Australia

314–321, 3rd Floor, Plot 3, Splendor Forum, Jasola District Centre, New Delhi – 110025, India

103 Penang Road, #05–06/07, Visioncrest Commercial, Singapore 238467

Cambridge University Press is part of Cambridge University Press & Assessment, a department of the University of Cambridge.

We share the University's mission to contribute to society through the pursuit of education, learning and research at the highest international levels of excellence.

www.cambridge.org
Information on this title: www.cambridge.org/9781009517263

DOI: 10.1017/9781009374163

First published 2024

A catalogue record for this publication is available from the British Library.

ISBN 978-1-009-51726-3 Hardback
ISBN 978-1-009-37415-6 Paperback
ISSN 2754-2955 (online)
ISSN 2754-2947 (print)

Ancient Maya Economies

Elements in Ancient and Pre-modern Economies

DOI: 10.1017/9781009374163
First published online: November 2024

Scott R. Hutson
University of Kentucky

Author for correspondence: Scott R. Hutson, scotthutson@uky.edu

Abstract: *Ancient Maya Economies* synthesizes the state of the art across seven components: geographical and historical background, ritual economy, households, specialization, exchange, political economies, and future directions. Other Elements case studies use many of the same components, making it easy to compare and contrast ancient Maya economies with systems of production and consumption in other parts of the world. The time is right for this Elements case because knowledge of ancient Maya economies has undergone a revolution in the last few decades, resulting in a complex panorama of new economic information. Aerial laser scanning has revealed higher amounts of intensive agriculture, and research on the ground has turned up better evidence for marketplaces. Maya economies feature specialized production, trade of both bulk goods and luxury goods, close integration with ritual and religion, and a carnival parade of political economies.

Keywords: marketplaces, craft specialization, ritual economy, household archaeology, ancient Maya

ISBNs: 9781009517263 (HB), 9781009374156 (PB), 9781009374163 (OC)
ISSNs: 2754-2955 (online), 2754-2947 (print)

Contents

1 Introduction

The ancient Maya are a group pre-Hispanic cultures native to Guatemala, Belize, eastern Mexico, and western Honduras and El Salvador (Figure 1). Along with the Mixtecs, Zapotecs, Toltecs, and others, they are part of Mesoamerica, a network of people whose frequent interactions resulted in shared and interlinked practices (farming maize, beans, and squash, playing ball), values (quadripartite worldview, sacrificial covenants), and institutions (ceremonial calendars). Unlike these other groups, however, if you Google the ancient Maya, your screen fills with high-profile documentaries from National Geographic, the History Channel, and other eager production companies. You may even stumble upon a blockbuster Hollywood film produced by Mel Gibson. The appetite for traveling museum exhibits of exquisite Maya artifacts is insatiable. If nothing else, the proof that the ancient Maya somehow resonate deeply with contemporary audiences lies in the fact that so many people in the year 2012 thought that a minor detail of a defunct Maya calendar system foreboded a twenty-first-century global cataclysm. The mystique of the ancient Maya originates from both truth – the Maya developed a remarkable writing system, stunning artistic canons, and advanced mathematical and astronomical knowledge – and fiction – the Maya refrained from violence and followed calendar priests untroubled by the dirty details of politics and poverty. Combined, these truths and fictions marked the Maya as exceptional.

At least fifty years have passed since mainstream, scientific archaeologists last touted the exceptionalism of the ancient Maya, but a fascination with the more rarefied aspects of Maya culture (royal palaces and hieroglyphic inscriptions) sometimes siphons attention away from the more mundane. I count economic activities – agriculture, craft production, and exchange – among the mundane. As Patricia McAnany (1993: 65) wrote thirty years ago: "[W]e have only very rudimentary notions about the economic organization of the Maya household and polity. This is due, in part, to the fact that we simply haven't been aggressively asking questions or structuring focused programs of inquiry regarding the Classic Maya economic system." Economics will always be a dismal science for Mayanists given that so much of what the ancient Maya produced and traded was perishable, including food and items made of materials – fiber, wood, gourds, and so on – that do not preserve well in the archaeological record. Thankfully, the growth of household archaeology and an explicit focus on marketplaces has boosted economic research over the past thirty years. Also, what we call economics was entangled with other spheres of life. Thus, it is no longer difficult to find book-length treatments of ancient Maya economies (McAnany 2010; King 2015a; Hutson 2017; Masson et al. 2020; Hutson & Golden 2024). This Element offers a short synthesis of the subject, including discussion of ritual

Figure 1 Map of the Maya area with locations mentioned in the text.

economy, households, agriculture, specialization, exchange, markets, and political economy. I focus primarily on the Lowlands and the Classic period (250–900 CE). While ancient Maya economies varied along a number of factors, including settlement size and degree of political centralization, a tentative generalization is possible: Ancient Maya economies consisted of high levels of household-based production of foodstuffs and craft goods in a tropical environment with relatively low settlement density, integrated and motivated by a rich spiritual life, strong social networks, and lively marketplaces. These economies sustained impressive monumental cities and noticeable social inequality in the absence of metal tools, beasts of burden, or wheeled transport. I begin by presenting the geographical and historical background of the ancient Maya.

2 Geographical and Historical Background

The rich history of the Maya spans over 3,000 years and many diverse ecotones. This review barely scratches the surface. For deeper accounts, I encourage readers to consult either of two accessible summaries: Coe and Houston (2022) or Sharer and Traxler (2006). The terrain occupied by the ancient Maya is often divided into two regions: Highlands and Lowlands. The tectonically active Sierra Madre mountain range, containing extinct and active volcanoes reaching nearly 4,000 m high, dominates the southern part of the Highlands. The northern part of the Highlands contains older metamorphic and igneous ranges such as the Cuchumatanes and Sierra de las Minas, rich in minerals such as jadeite and serpentine. A bit to the north in the Alta Verapaz region we find lower, younger, but no less dramatic karst topography, which eventually grades northward to the flatter limestone shelf of the Lowlands. Uplift has raised this limestone shelf above sea level over the last thirty million years, with the northern section emerging most recently. Thus, the younger northern segment is flatter and lower. Rainwater quickly drains to the water table through cracks in the bedrock and other openings where limestone has dissolved. The water table is close to the surface, however, providing year-round access to water through natural solution features locally called "cenotes." The Southern Lowland region is higher and more eroded and features rivers flowing into the Gulf of Mexico and the Caribbean as well as poorly drained basins, called "bajos," that flood during the rainy season. Monsoons cause pronounced wet and dry seasons in both the Highlands and the Lowlands, occurring at the same time: wet from approximately May to November, with peak rainfall in June and October. The boundary between the Northern and Southern Lowlands is blurry and straddled in part by the elevated interior region, which has no year-round water sources due to a lack of rivers and a water table too low to be reached by wells or solution features. By selectively focusing mostly on sites in the northern reaches of the Northern Lowlands (ruins like Chichen Itza, Coba, and Dzibilchaltun) and sites much further south (ruins like Tikal, Uaxactun, Ceibal, and Belizean sites), archaeologists have left a void of largely unstudied areas in southern Campeche and southern Quintana Roo (with the exception of sites like Becan and Xpujil near Mexico's highway 186), artificially concretizing the boundary between the Northern Lowlands and the rest of the Lowlands. Yet the distinction between Northern and Southern/Central Lowlands retains cultural significance as it appears that 1,200 years ago the Northern Lowland Maya spoke mostly Yucatec, while Lowlanders to the south spoke other Maya languages such as Classic Ch'olti'an (the language of the inscriptions) and precursors to Western Ch'olan languages such as Ch'ol and Chontal.

Vegetation, temperature, and annual rainfall vary dramatically within both the Highlands and the Lowlands. Unsurprisingly, temperature varies by elevation, with parts of the Highlands averaging less than 15°C over the year with occasional frosts and parts of the Mexican state of Tabasco, in the Lowlands, averaging 28°C. Natural vegetation in the Highlands consists of a mix of deciduous and evergreen forests, with oak, pine, cypress, juniper, and laurel. The area around Palenque, Mexico, the Middle Usumacinta River valley, and southern Belize receive over 3,000 mm (sometimes over 4,000 mm) of rain per year, whereas the northwestern segment of the Northern Lowlands and highland valleys like the Middle Motagua receive less than 1,000 mm annually. In the Lowlands, precipitation generally decreases from south to north. Though heavily deforested over the past decades and of course partly deforested by ancient farmers, the Southern and Central Lowlands contain lush tropical forests (predominant trees include cedar, mahogany, sapodilla, and ceiba in the high canopy and palms, rubber, breadnut and allspice lower down), which grade to shrub forests in the drier, northern tip of the Peninsula.

The word Maya can be used to refer to a contemporary population of over seven million people, living in cities and countrysides of Mesoamerica and diasporic communities in the United States and Europe. They share familiarity with a Maya language, of which there are over thirty. Hieroglyphic decipherment shows that the language written by Maya scribes over 1,000 years ago is ancestral to or related to contemporary Maya languages. Maya speakers across time exhibit remarkable cultural resilience, having endured pre-Hispanic political and demographic disruption, Spanish colonization and genocide, postcolonial oppression, and absorption of newcomers (enslaved and otherwise) from other parts of the world.

The earliest Maya, possible speakers of what linguists call Proto-Mayan, began producing pottery and building monumental architecture as early as 3,000 years ago at sites like Aguada Fenix, Mexico, and Ceibal, Guatemela (Inomata et al. 2020). Whereas these builders may not yet have lived in houses year-round, potters of similar antiquity in what is now Belize appear to have built houses first and then, a few generations later, began erecting larger, public structures. People in the Maya area began eating maize much earlier than the first evidence of pottery and sedentary villages (Kennett et al. 2020), and maize was not a dominant crop even for these first villagers. In addition to maize, there are other signs of similarities between the first villagers and their preceramic, non-sedentary forebears, such as continuity of stone tool traditions (Lohse 2020). It is therefore not so easy to pinpoint the beginnings of Maya cultures. The beginnings of pottery in the Maya area, a full 500 years later than Mesoamerican neighbors, mark the Early Middle Preclassic (1000–700 BCE).

The Late Middle Preclassic, spanning about 700–400 BCE, saw a homogenization of pottery styles across the Lowlands as well as the spread of monumental construction, often in the form of what has been called the "E-Group": a compound consisting of a square pyramid on the west and a low, north/south-oriented structure on the east. Some E-groups were oriented to astronomical phenomena. Political and economic organizations in the Middle Preclassic are rather opaque. Monumental construction appears to precede appreciable inequality but might imply "cosmo-political" inequality between humans and nonhuman persons.

The Late Preclassic, from 400 BCE to 250 CE, witnessed an uptick in monumental construction at sites like El Mirador, Calakmul, and Yaxuna. The people at most major settlements built triadic groups: complexes that included three temples atop a large basal platform and were more exclusive than earlier E-Groups. This shift toward exclusive ritual coincides with some of the first indications of dynastic rulership, including remarkable murals at San Bartolo, Guatemala, showing a scene of enthronement, and carved stela in the Mirador Basin. A network of causeways emanating from El Mirador and linking with secondary centers may indicate regional statecraft. El Mirador collapsed at the end of the Late Preclassic, due in part to deforestation. Tikal, on the other hand, established its first ruling dynasty in the Late Preclassic and transitioned smoothly into the Early Classic (250– 600 CE).

For sites like Tikal that thrived in both the Late Preclassic and the Early Classic, the difference between these two periods is minor, consisting mostly of the use of the long count calendar (a calendar that tallies the number of days elapsed since a mythical beginning point which in our calendar equates to 3114 BCE) and greater visibility of rulers as unique individuals with names and biographies displayed on various media. Rulers in the Classic period presided over city-states spread like a lattice across the Lowlands. Similar to Classical Greek city states, Maya city states ranged in population from a few thousand to figures in the lower six digits. This range is important as we will see that large city state capitals, such as Tikal, Caracol, and Calakmul, had more complex economies. Each city state whose ruler possessed the *k'uhul ajaw* (holy lord) title was nominally independent. Yet some city-states were more powerful than others and at various times in the Classic period, overlords headed alliances of multiple city-states. While leaders of powerful kingdoms like Calakmul and Tikal could intervene in the political affairs of lesser, client kingdoms, they never formed empires and lacked the bureaucracy to take over the administration of subject kingdoms. In some parts of the Maya world, the *k'uhul ajaw* title has not been documented, leading to the possibility of collective forms of governance as opposed to dynastic monarchy. Polities with *k'uhul ajaws* likely also contained collective features such as councils of different sorts. In many cases, rural terrain in between city state capitals was not carefully marked with sharp territorial borders. The reach of a city state fluctuated based on the continually negotiated personal and political relationships between the ruler and potential subjects.

As Mesoamericans, the Maya interacted with other Mesoamerican cultures, including the Olmec in the Preclassic period, the Toltecs in the Terminal Classic period, and artists and merchants sharing in the Mixteca Puebla style of Central Mexico during the Late Postclassic. Highland and Lowland Maya were in contact with the people of the Great Central Mexican city of Teotihuacan at least as early as the third century CE and these interactions intensified in the late fourth century when a contingent of warriors affiliated with Teotihuacan interrupted the dynastic sequence at Tikal and other cities.

By the Late Classic period (600–900 CE), the Maya world reached its peak population. Settlement densities calculated on the basis of extensive airborne laser scanning (also called lidar: Light Detection and Ranging) in the Lowlands suggests a plausible figure of eighty people per km^2, amounting to a population of about fifteen million people for the 190,000 km^2 that comprise the Lowlands. By the end of the Classic period, most Maya city-states in the Central and Southern Lowlands experienced drastic population loss and a collapse of centralized political institutions. Different circumstances played into these declines in different areas, but common challenges include drought, increased warfare, environmental degradation, and disillusionment with extractive and increasingly numerous nobles. The ensuing Postclassic period featured less-hierarchical societies and reconfigured trade routes. After a wave of smallpox and other Old World diseases and an alliance of Spaniards, Tarascans, and other natives of Central Mexico toppled the Aztecs in 1521, the conquistadors turned their focus to the Maya Highlands, befriending the Kaqchikel kingdom in order to subdue the K'iche and Tz'utujil in 1524. After failed attempts to control the Northern Lowlands, the Spanish established a partial hegemony in 1547 with the founding of the colonial city of Merida on top of the Maya city of Tiho'. Yet the eastern side of the peninsula received very little attention from Spaniards and was not incorporated into the Mexican nation state until the twentieth century. To the south, in the vicinity of Tikal, the Maya kingdom of Peten Itza did not accept Spanish missionaries, nor [nominal] Spanish control until 1697.

3 Embeddedness

Most archaeologists study the ancient Maya within an anthropological framework. We therefore view economics as inseparable from the institutions, habits, and worldviews that structure life more generally. This approach differs starkly from Adam Smith's argument that economics is a distinct domain, largely untethered from governments and other institutions, and therefore an independent "field of human inquiry with its own principles and laws" (Graeber 2011: 25). Anthropology's early heritage of studying "exotic" societies peripheral to capitalist market systems predisposed many of its practitioners to insist that economic activities were "embedded" in cultural logics often alien to principles of rational maximization (Polanyi 1944). Anthropologists toeing this line were called substantivists, in contrast to formalists, who were said to be more in line with Smith's view that maximization of benefits and minimization of costs drive human behavior, independent of cultural context.

In the end, the dichotomy between substantivism and formalism crumbles because it establishes a false polarity between superrational, self-gain obsessed, "modern" people and reactionary, custom-bound, self-sacrificial traditionalists. Substantivism may frame people as kindhearted and moral as opposed to ruthless opportunists born to truck and barter, yet it denies them the ability to act strategically and advocate for change. As ethnographer Ted Fischer (1999) has shown, a cultural logic like the cosmological centrality of soul (*k'u'x*) and spirit (*anima*) does indeed guide Highland (Kaqchikel) Maya senses of self, but also serves as a resource that contemporary activists draw on to forge broader, pan-ethnic Maya identities that are most effective in countering government policies that oppress indigenous groups. Stated differently, people can be deeply committed to the unique substance of their culture while at the same time refashioning it in order to seize opportunities and avoid exploitation.

If substantivism fails because it sees actors in traditional societies as too heavily constrained by cultural, institutional, and social forces, formalism falters because it sees actors in modernized market societies as too atomized, autonomous, and unmoored from cultural, institutional, and social forces. In the most cited of all sociology publications, Mark Granovetter (1985: 494) tackles a question that has been debated in different versions going back to Hobbes: If economic actors "pursue their own advantage with all means at their command, including guile and deceit," what prevents a market from devolving into a war of all against all? More simply, how do exchange partners build trust? A Hobbesian would respond that institutions emerge to eliminate fraud and malfeasance by regulatory fiat. Yet regulatory arrangements are a poor substitute for trust and only encourage creative and novel forms of evasion and duplicity (Granovetter 1985: 491). The alternative response, which rings of substantivism, is that people are somehow trustworthy by nature. Indeed, all societies have some form of morality, but Granovetter finds that economies don't work only from a pre-given reservoir of trust. His analysis of corporate behavior shows that trust is built and rebuilt from ongoing social relations. For the ancient Maya, Golden and Scherer (2013) make a very similar point. Indeed, social relations between suppliers, buyers, contractors, and others lead to deals that do not always maximize profit.

In sum, capitalist and precapitalist societies share a key similarity: Economic relations are embedded in social relations. Understanding the embeddedness of ancient Maya economies therefore requires a deeper look at social relations. This deeper look reveals that the ancient Maya retained a rather broad set of social relations. Like most indigenous groups of the Americas, the Maya are animist: Nonhumans can be persons, and what we see as inanimate objects can be alive. Discussing the highland Maya of Guatemala, ethnographer Sol Tax (1941: 38) wrote that "sun and earth, river and hill, are anthropomorphized; animals talk; plants have emotions; it is possible for a hoe to work alone; such things as fire and maize are capable of direct punitive action." Social relations therefore encompass a broad spectrum of beings. This holds for the Classic period as well (Harrison-Buck 2012; Houston 2014). The Maya are also monist, meaning that entities that we would sort out as sacred or profane all belong to the same (and only) order of being (Astor-Aguilera 2010: 6). Thus, "deities" are quite down-to-earth and approachable. Yet social relations between humans and other-than-human beings are hierarchical. The Maya owe debts to deities who created humans and the world they occupy and to ancestors from whom humans inherit land, livelihoods, and identity. Patricia McAnany's (2010) term "ancestral economy" aptly refers to the way in which Maya economies entangle with obligations to forebears and other beings.

Such obligations, which John Monaghan (2000) glosses as "covenants" in order to capture their cosmological gravity, play out on a day-to-day basis. They seamlessly intermingle "mundane" activities, such as farming, hunting, and potting, with what we would call other-worldly activities: prayer, burning incense, and making offerings. Looking more closely at farming, hunting, and potting highlights the lack of bounds between domains that analysts often keep separate: economics and ritual.

Regarding farming, Redfield and Villa Rojas (1962: 127) wrote of the Yucatec Maya: "What man wins from nature, he takes from the gods." This makes clear that, before anything else, farming is a moral relationship with supernaturals, in this case the guardian spirits of the forest, to whom farmers make multiple offerings. When clearing a forest plot, farmers clear only the precise amount of land needed. Though rational, this logic is also moral because trees are sentient; chopping too many of them betrays the covenant between farmer and guardian spirit and breaks the promise that the guardian spirit made to the trees. Thus, when a farmer sustains injury while felling trees, Redfield and Villa Rojas' informants (1962: 134) suspect that the farmer offended the guardians of the forest. Cosmology also helps explain the rectangular shape of the plot. A rectangle is rational in that it allows easier measurement of land but to the Yucatec Maya farmer, this shape is basic to the frame of reference in which all aspects of his life are lived (Hanks 1990). The notion that the world is divided into four parts, with four corners, anchors Yucatecan cosmology and phenomenology. In Maya myths, the world itself was created as a four-cornered place and, in contemporary times, centering the self in a four-cornered world is a prerequisite for proper life.

Hunting is also embedded in various social relations. Brown and Emery's (2008: 304) study of Highland Maya hunting shows that "animate beings of various ontological statuses – human, wild animals, spirit guardians, topographic features, dogs, weapons and skeletal remains – must maintain engaged relations based on commensality and mutual respect to avoid negative repercussions." More specifically, if hunters satisfy a network of obligations to these different agents through offerings, communication, only taking the proper amount of prey, and bringing the bones of previous prey back to the hunting shrines, new prey will sacrifice themselves to hunters. Regarding pottery, Highland Maya potters see clay as a living being that resists their attempts to manipulate it, requiring rituals that enlist spirits in helping to control the clay and other raw materials (Reina & Hill 1978: 232–6).

The repeated communication with other-than-human beings amounts to the notion of ritualized production. For example, the Lacandon Maya observed various rites before and during the process of making stone tools, including fasting and chanting to the flint (Clark 1989). They also needed to knap flint inside temples. Likewise, Yucatec Maya wood carvers in the sixteenth century endured taboos and rites as part of the production process (Tozzer 1941:159–60). With the blurred line between sacred and profane, however, the Maya do not see such production steps as rites. It is all work, falling, among the Yucatec, under a single term (*meyaj*). I should also mention that an ancestral economy involves the investment of a significant amount of effort and resources into making the goods (food, incense, and pottery) used as offerings in various stages of work.

Admittedly, a long history of postcolonial discrimination, the dislocations of colonialism, and the turmoil of the Classic to Postclassic transition separates the Classic period Maya from these examples of farming, hunting, and toolmaking. Yet archaeology does provide glimpses of the principles of embeddedness discussed thus far. For example, Aoyama (1995) found evidence at the Copan acropolis that suggests that artisans made blood offerings while working hides and crafting objects of shell and wood. At Chunchucmil, ancient households' preference for depositing trash on the west side of their houselots reveals the ways in which the symbolism of the quadripartite world shaped daily activities; practical maintenance was embedded in cultural logic (Hutson & Stanton 2007). While this section of the Element has focused on how economic activities were embedded in relations with other-than-human beings, ancient Maya economies were also embedded in human relations (for example, exchanges that take the form of balanced reciprocity) and politics (for instance, government sponsorship of marketplaces). The household is the most basic institution of economic relations, as described in the following section.

4 Household Economy

Households are groups of people who share in most, but not always all, of the following activities: production, consumption, co-residence, pooling of resources, and social and physical reproduction (Ashmore & Wilk 1988). Household archaeology is a major facet of research on the ancient Maya (Hendon 1991; Robin 2013; Masson & Peraza Lope 2014; Ardren et al. 2016; Sheets 2020; Triadan & Inomata 2020). Given the scarcity of what we might call factories and large business corporations in the ancient Maya world, households were the basic economic institution. Decisions of what and how much to produce were made by the women, men, and children of each household. Saying that households were a basic unit does not mean that households were fully independent. For example, households gained political clout as part of larger corporate groups such as neighborhoods. Furthermore, I will argue later that households were not self-sufficient; they met their needs through various forms of exchange. Kinship structures and norms that influenced where new couples would reside shaped, to some degree, membership in ancient Maya households. Nevertheless, given that households were at the core of social, economic, and political transformations, archaeologists pay less attention to membership criteria and more attention to what households do.

Research on the material signature of an ancient Maya household normally targets domestic compounds whose elements encompass several household activities. Houses index co-residence, shrines suggest social reproduction, kitchens and storage structures indicate consumption and pooling of resources. These buildings often line the sides of a shared patio that encouraged the kinds of social interactions which boost social reproduction but also accommodate various productive activities, such as craftwork. Gardens and economically useful trees usually surround the structural core and patio and the existence of such cultivated spaces within towns and cities contributed to relatively low settlement densities. Figure 2(a) depicts an idealized historic period houselot. Though it was once common to assume that the domestic realm was private and gendered female, residential compounds up and down the social hierarchy were also men's work places and public spaces in which men, women, and children from beyond the household met and shared food.

Households consist of both nuclear families, detectible by the presence of domestic compounds with a single residence, and extended families, who occupy compounds with multiple separate residences (usually each residence is its own discrete building). At many archaeological sites, excavations reveal a cycle of growth from nuclear to extended families in which the first stage of occupation contains a single residence and later stages contain multiple residences as children of the founding couple establish their own homes within the domestic compound (Haviland 1988). In extended family households, there is often a household head who lives in the most elaborate residence. Figure 2(b) shows archaeological examples of domestic compounds pertaining to extended family households of various sizes. Extended family households with more people provided the agency and flexibility of scheduling to engage in a variety of enterprises, including farming, crafting, and extraction of raw materials. Domestic structures (Figure 3) – often called housemounds because most are constructed on top of elevated stone platforms – vastly outnumber other sorts of buildings (temples, ballcourts, and administrative structures). Since natural formation processes have not yet buried ancient platforms in many parts of the Maya world, housemounds are still ubiquitous today. While some residential compounds were constructed of entirely perishable material and are not easily visible to archaeologists, relatively accurate demographic calculations can be made on the basis of detailed surface mapping and test pitting to see which houses were occupied at the same time. Given that the Maya were an agrarian society, any treatment of household economies must explore the primary productive activity: farming.

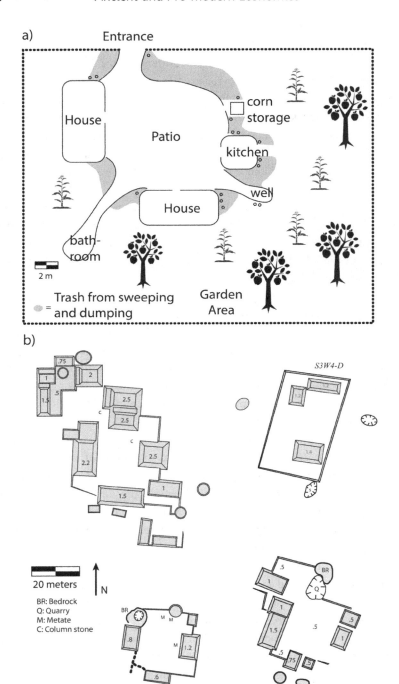

Figure 2 (a) Idealized houselot model. (b) Plans of domestic compounds from Chunchucmil, Yucatan.

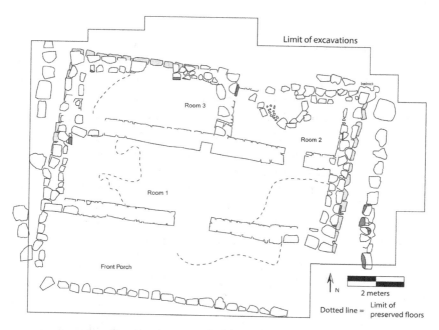

Figure 3 (a) Plan view of an excavated house (Str. S2E2-22) from Chunchucmil, Yucatan. (b) Photo of the same house, looking northeastward.

4.1 Agriculture

In the Classic period, maize was the primary crop, followed by beans, squash, chilies, and manioc. The centrality of maize in Maya iconography and mythology reflects the importance of this food in both livelihoods and cosmology (Taube 2018). Maize entered the diet as early as 4,700 years ago and in some places comprised a substantial portion of the diet only a millennium afterward (Kennett et al. 2020). Ancient Maya farmers did not use plows and had no beasts of burden to pull them. With a few exceptions (such as the Perdidio reservoir at Tikal [Scarborough & Grazioso Sierra 2015: 33] or the springhouse at Chan, Belize [Wyatt 2012]), they also did not use irrigation. Most farmers depended on rainfall. Based on analogy with farming techniques used by twentieth-century Maya of Northern Yucatan, archaeologists once assumed that the ancient Maya practiced long-fallow swidden and little else. In this "slash and burn" system, a farmer fells trees in a forest plot rarely larger than a hectare or two, allows the sun to parch the downed vegetation through the dry season, and then burns it shortly before the rains come. The farmer then plants seeds with a digging stick. Unaided by fertilizer, cultivators might replant the plot the following year before allowing the land to go fallow for a decade or more and moving on to slash another parcel (Highland soils often accommodate five to ten consecutive annual crops before fallowing). This form of agriculture is extensive as opposed to intensive, requiring lots of land and minimal (if any) landscape modification. The long-fallow system supports low populations but is well adapted to the thin soils of the relatively flat Northern Lowlands. On the other hand, it is not as well adapted to the more varied topography of the Southern and Central Lowlands where slash and burn can lead to erosion on sloped terrain and does not work in the slow-draining seasonal wetlands.

In the 1960s and 1970s, two developments challenged the slash and burn orthodoxy: (1) Settlement pattern studies showed that Classic period population densities in some areas were too high to be supported by long-fallow swidden; and (2) researchers found evidence of intensive forms of agriculture such as wetland fields and terracing. Additional research documented several other forms of intensive agriculture or associated features, such as arboriculture, polyculture, kitchen gardens, reservoirs, stone field walls, and utilization of moist sinkholes and margins of basins enriched by eroded sediment. This profusion of agricultural techniques led to the "managed mosaic" model, in which ancient landscapes are understood to exhibit remarkable heterogeneity (a mosaic) and Maya farmers matched this heterogeneity with just as diverse an array of management strategies (Fedick 1996). Farmers accumulated hard-won knowledge of local growing conditions (drainage, soil fertility, variation in weather, and particular needs of individual species) and passed it down to subsequent generations. Many ancient Maya farmers did indeed use slash and burn agriculture and it is important to recognize that plots lying fallow provided foods and household items of all sorts. Secondary growth should be seen as a forest garden, not just forest (Ford 2020). In the last decades, extensive remote sensing (lidar in particular) and ground verification (including survey and excavation) have provided a better sense of the scale of intensive agricultural features and which ones were most common. I focus on the two best documented forms of intensive agriculture: terraces and wetland fields.

4.1.1 Terraces

The ancient Maya used stone terraces to create relatively flat planting surfaces on hilly terrain (Figure 4). Terraces impound sediment, therefore reducing erosion and creating deeper soils in which corn, beans, and squash but also root crops can thrive. Terraces also slow the flow of water, increasing moisture on the planting surfaces and once again lessening erosion (Chase & Weishampel 2016; MacCrae & Iannone 2016). Archaeologists have documented several kinds of terraces. The three most common are terraces on hillsides that run parallel to natural slope contours, cross-channel terraces (also called weir

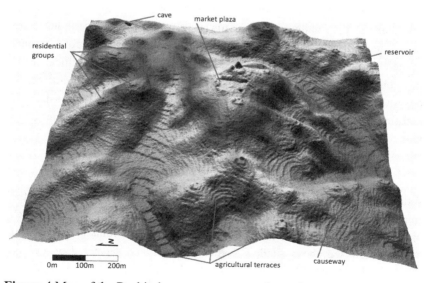

Figure 4 Map of the Puchituk causeway area at Caracol, showing terraces and other features. Adapted from figure 5 of Chase et al. 2012, used with permission of the authors.

terraces and check dams), and footslope terraces. Terraces are widespread in west-central and northwest Belize, southern Quintana Roo, Mexico, and southeastern Campeche, Mexico. They are less common in the Peten district of Guatemala. They were first documented in Campeche and Quintana Roo in the 1930s, and Turner's research in the 1970s suggested that the Maya built terraces across 10,000 km^2 in this region (Turner 1974). Lidar mapping that expands Turner's survey coverage by a factor of about a thousand suggests that terracing can indeed be found across nearly 10,000 km^2 in this part of Mexico at a density of about 100 linear meters per hectare (Hutson et al. 2021a). The area with the highest density of terracing is on the Vaca Plateau of west-central Belize at sites such as Waybil (nearly 1,300 linear meters of terracing per hectare) and Caracol (about 600 linear meters per hectare).

The configuration of terraces and other linear features can tell us something about the organization of agricultural production. At Caracol, the vast scale and uniform spacing of terraces have led Chase and Chase (1998: 73) to suggest the existence of centralized management. At the same time, impressive wet-rice terrace systems in Ifugao (Philippines) and Bali result not from centralized intervention but village-level work groups and self-organizing processes (Acabado 2013). In terraced areas of southern Quintana Roo, Mexico, terraces link with berms to form linear features that pass by several domestic compounds and extend for over a kilometer. The construction of these features required cooperation between households, but does not imply intervention from above. In this context, the smallholder model fits best (Pyburn 1998). Smallholders are enterprising cultivators whose intensive agricultural inputs allow for a surplus not merely to mitigate subsistence risks or withstand extractive political economies but, perhaps, to enrich their social networks, engage in commerce, or boost quality of life. The enhanced value of the farmland and the prospect of inheriting it incentivizes younger generations to stick around and contribute labor.

4.1.2 Wetland Fields

Wetland agriculture in the Maya area takes many forms. One form resembles the remarkably productive chinampas from the Basin of Mexico that fed the Aztec capital of Tenochtitlan and continue to be farmed today. Chinampas consist of small fields raised above shallow bodies of water and separated by canals. Farmers dug nutrient-rich muck from the canals and piled it on the raised fields as fertilizer. The high-quality water in the canals supports fish and mollusks. Chinampa-like wetland fields have been documented at Chawak But'o'ob, Belize (Beach et al. 2019). They were once thought to be more widespread in the Maya area but many potential examples turned out to be nonanthropogenic. More common are drained fields, in which rising water tables threaten to make land uncultivable, spurring farmers to dig channels to drain off water. The scale of infrastructure at places like the Birds of Paradise fields in Northern Belize (Figure 5), whose interconnected drainage canals cover 7.7 km^2, suggests more inter-household cooperation than the terrace systems. One farmer's terraces can succeed even if a farmer upslope builds sloppy terraces. However, successfully drawing away water across multiple square kilometers requires coordination between all the farmers in the wetland.

A conclusion of several recent studies of terracing and wetland agriculture is that the ancient Maya produced food surpluses in less densely populated areas and transported these surpluses to more densely populated areas (Canuto et al. 2018; Beach et al. 2019: 21474; Hutson et al. 2021a). Similar conclusions have been made in the Northern Lowlands where intensive agriculture leaves more subtle marks (Masson & Freidel 2013). The form of exchange is equivocal but likely involved a mixture of political economy, whereby farmers delivered surplus food to cities as tax or tribute, and commercial economy, where marketplaces in cities incentivized surplus production by offering farmers a chance to accumulate rare goods in exchange for their bounty in crops. Maya city state capitals lacked the kind of extensive bulk storehouses seen at Inca administrative centers, suggesting less control over agricultural production. The construction of terraces at Chan in Belize during the Middle Preclassic (Wyatt 2012), a time and place where markets, tribute demands, and land shortages all seem unlikely, suggests that an impetus behind intensive farming was to build and maintain social relations through sharing surplus food. There is no clear correlation between settlement density and landesque capital: some locations with concentrated population (Caracol) have extensive evidence of intensive agriculture, whereas other areas with concentrated population and conditions that would favor intensive agriculture in the form of terracing (such as the Puuc region and Tikal) lack major terracing (Dunning et al. 2020).

Based on analogy with nonmechanized agriculture in twentieth-century Yucatan, Mexico, archaeologists often assumed men farmed. Yet due to colonial-era Spanish policies that resettled Yucatecan farmers from the countryside to villages and towns, farmers had to travel longer distances to "outfield" plots. Among groups like the Lacandon, where agroforestry plots were rarely more than 1.5 km away from houses, entire families (men, women, and children) worked in the fields (Robin 2006). Since most ancient terraces in the Maya area are quite close to houses, it is likely that women and children also worked these fields prior to Spanish contact. Robin (2006) notes that gendered imagery from both the Classic and Postclassic periods suggests that both men and women participated in farming.

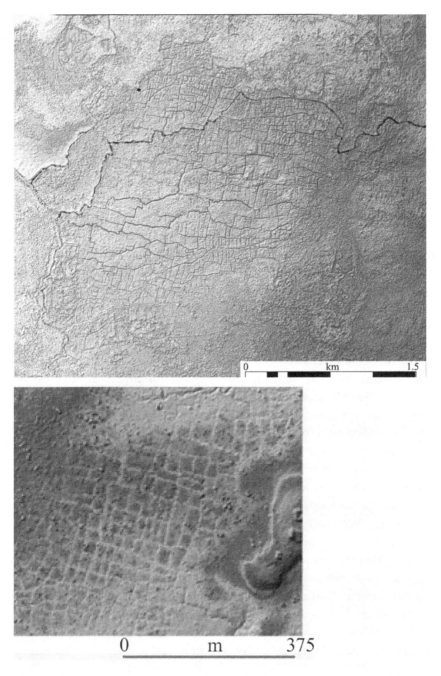

Figure 5 (a) and (b) Birds of Paradise wetland fields, Belize. Adapted from Beach et al. 2019, used with permission of the authors.

4.2 Land Ownership

Did farmers own the land they cultivated? If so, could they sell it? Or was land owned communally? A lack of written records regarding land tenure systems among the ancient Maya makes these questions difficult to answer. Nevertheless, ethnohistoric documents from the colonial period and archaeological details permit speculation. In sixteenth-century Yucatan, families owned assets such as houses and houselots, which were heritable (Farriss 1984). The houselot consists of an architectural core whose buildings (residences, kitchens, storage structures, and shrines) normally delimit a patio (Figure 2). Beyond the core (and the ring of debris that usually accumulates at its edge) lies the largest part of the houselot, a zone with gardens, economically useful trees, and occasional work areas. Walls delimit the boundaries of houselots in ethnographic, colonial, and, occasionally, precolonial cases. Produce, medicine, and other materials from the garden zone made important contributions to subsistence, but at sites with well-known houselot boundary walls (Coba, Mayapan, Chunchucmil), the space within the houselot was far too small to provision the household (Hutson et al. 2021b). Thus, houselot gardens were heritable, but these account for only a small percentage of the total productive land.

Beyond the houselot, the ethnohistoric sources imply that farmland was the property of the community at large though specific trees could be inherited along the female line. However, a family that made improvements to land owned those improvements (LeCount et al. 2019). Farmers are not likely to invest heavily in land without the assurance that they would gain some form of long-term entitlement. Thus, it is likely that Maya terraced fields were "owned" by their cultivators. Drained wetland fields might be different. Since large field systems like Birds of Paradise, Belize, require coordinated labor of multiple households, they might be owned communally. Alternatively, since nobles may have owned private estates (Roys 1943) and since slavery was an important source of labor at the time of Spanish Contact, large tracts of landesque capital may have been owned by nobles and improved by their chattel. McAnany and colleagues (2002) make the case that cacao orchards were controlled by royalty. In southern Quintana Roo and Campeche during the Classic period and in Northeastern Quintana Roo in the Postclassic period (Figure 1), stone walls enclosed thousands of parcels of land. Partitioning of land implies private ownership, and Batun and colleagues (2020) have explored complex forms of ownership in the Contact period. If the subdivisions are approximately the same size, they could be communal (LeCount et al. 2019). Enclosed agricultural plots at the coastal Quintana Roo sites of Calica, San Gervasio, and Xelha contain close to 4,000 m^2 on average, but the large amount of variation in plot size (only about two thirds of the plots fall between 2,000 m^2 to 6,000 m^2) implies a lack of standardization, and therefore private ownership.

4.3 Inequality

Inequality between households is important for many reasons. High levels of inequality lead to inefficiencies and instabilities that imperil growth and threaten social cohesion. At the same time, under the right circumstances, inequality can contribute to social vibrancy and increased productivity. When people of diverse wealth levels are interspersed throughout cities, opportunities for interaction and mixing provide chances for contacts and exchange of ideas that could lead to economic, social, political, or other opportunities (Glaeser 2011). Thus, two important questions arise: How much inequality was there between ancient Maya households and to what degree did unequal households intermingle?

Before getting to these questions, let's define inequality and consider how to measure it. Two common approaches to inequality among the ancient Maya are wealth and status. Fewer scholars consider class, and when doing so, they avoid the structural Marxist perspective in which class depends on whether a person gives up surplus, collects surplus, or receives surplus from those who collect it. Wealth refers to the amount of labor and goods at one's disposal. Status can refer to genealogical pedigree, intimacy with supernatural forces, control of knowledge, and more. The two concepts overlap since intimacy with supernatural forces may require the goods necessary to make extraordinary offerings and the labor necessary to construct large shrines and temples. Yet they are distinct in the sense that not all high-status people are wealthy. I turn to the 9N-8 architectural compound at Copan as an example. Several discrete households occupied 9N-8, which has about fifty buildings arranged around multiple courtyards. The fact that many courtyards had their own kitchen, shrine, and domiciles suggests that each courtyard accommodated a household. There was clear inequality among these households. At the end of the eighth century, the occupants of structure 9N-82c stood well above the others in the 9N-8 compound in terms of both wealth (for example, 9N-82c required over 10,000 person days to construct and is located in the largest courtyard with the most imposing temple) and status (9N-82c contained a hieroglyphic inscription identifying the owner as Mak'an Chanal, a scribe [Maya scribes possessed highly valued skills and cosmological knowledge] who out-ranked everyone at Copan except king Yax Pasaj Chan Yopaat). In comparison, several households had modest possessions and lived in buildings requiring a fiftieth of the labor summoned for 9N-82c. Although these low-wealth households may have functioned essentially as servants (Hendon 1991: 912), being part of the House of Mak'an Chanal bolstered their status, making them minor elites. The case of 9N-8 also shows that we can't always consider ancient Maya societies as an atomized array of households. Households can be members of larger units from which they derive status and with whom wealth is pooled.

Measuring inequality systematically across large cities requires focusing on wealth as opposed to status. The archaeological signatures of status include personal adornment, mortuary offerings, hieroglyphic statements of parentage, tools of ritual specialists, and more. Yet systematic recovery of these presumes a research design – extensive excavation across a large sample of residential groups – that is too expensive for most archaeology projects. On the other hand, proxies for wealth – area and volume of residential structures – can be collected through less expensive methods: mapping of residences and extensive but small excavations (test pits) to determine which houses were contemporaneous. Admittedly, there are problems with using house size as a proxy for wealth. Yet archaeologists commonly deploy this proxy because ethnographers have confirmed a rough correlation between wealth and house size both in the Maya area and in other agrarian contexts (Wilk 1983; Smith 1987). Furthermore, extensive excavations in the Maya area often find that bigger houses contain artifacts of greater quality and broader variety.

One of the clearest results of the analysis of variation in house size is that at sites with a large number (over 100) of residential compounds, households fail to sort into wealth classes. In other words, variation is continuous such that if house sizes were arranged from smallest to largest, as in a Lorenz curve, there are no breakpoints separating, for example, "elite" households from the rest (Hutson 2020). Other patterns emerge when considering overall degrees of inequality as calculated using Gini coefficients. The Gini coefficient is a measure of inequality that ranges between 0 (full equality, in which all households have identical resources) and 1 (complete inequality, in which one household has all the resources and the others have none). Gini scores for architectural volume in the Maya area range from about 0.5 to 0.63, while Gini scores for surface area range from about 0.3 to 0.45 (Thompson et al. 2021). To put this in context, the mean of an ethnographic sample of foragers is 0.25, the mean of an ethnographic sample of intensive agriculturalists is 0.57 (Shenk et al. 2010), and the Gini coefficients of modern cities range quite widely, from 0.2 to 0.7. These comparisons are somewhat uninformative, however, since the Gini coefficients from beyond the Maya area do not all look at architecture. Comparing a Gini coefficient for house size with a Gini coefficient for income, for example, may be like comparing apples and oranges.

Examining Gini scores on a single variable (surface area of houses) from a range of cities in Mesoamerica has suggested to some researchers that more autocratic polities have greater inequality while more collective polities have less inequality. The pattern is complicated, however, for two reasons. First, archaeologists attribute (at least) two distinct meanings to the term "collective": (1) polities where governments extract critical resources from their own subjects; and (2) polities where many different groups and individuals participate in decision-making. In this Element, I use the latter meaning. Second, published studies often compare settlements that vary greatly in size, chronology, and environmental context, and sometimes use two different variables and misreport actual Gini scores (Kohler et al. 2018). Better-controlled comparisons suggest a lack of correlation between wealth inequality and the degree of autocratic governance.

In the last forty years, Amartya Sen (a Nobel Prize winner in Economics) and others have suggested that analysts should not measure inequality by wealth alone. The ancient Maya had choices regarding where to invest their energy, and while some households chose to pursue wealth, it is clear that others did not (Sheets 2020; Hutson 2023). Competing values structured decisions about what goals to pursue. Many households achieved a sense of well-being not by accumulating what we believe are proxies for wealth (exotic portable goods and large houses) but by commitment to community service or supernatural beings or some other fulfilling task, such as craftwork.

In any event, measures of wealth and well-being confirm what any tourist who has wandered through a palace-strewn ruin can infer: Maya cities harbored a substantial amount of inequality. Did spatial layouts segregate the rich and the poor? Or did urban design facilitate chance encounters between people of widely different backgrounds? Different cities exhibit different patterns. A few cities exhibit even mixing of rich and poor households. More commonly, the richest and most powerful households tend to be located near the site core, but less wealthy households were nearly always interspersed among them. Contact between such households may have been structured in a variety of ways and neighborhood, house, or lineage identity might crosscut household differences. Yet the lack of spatial segregation in Maya sites ensured opportunities for the kind of social mixing said to boost urban economies (Bettencourt & West 2010).

5 Craft Specialization

Household archaeology in the form of extensive excavations of domestic compounds has shed light on debates about self-sufficiency. Were Maya households able to supply all of their basic needs, or did they depend drastically on exchange? Or something in between (Masson & Freidel 2012)? Did urban and rural households exhibit similar degrees of interdependency? Archaeologists normally approach these questions by looking at household production. What we find in the Maya world is that, rather than every household doing everything, some specialize. This section therefore explores craft specialization. Before defining specialized production, I warn readers that formation processes of the archaeological record often make our data dismally deficient. The ancient Maya worked mostly with biodegradable materials. Preservation conditions have erased wood, textiles, hides, fuel, fruits, seeds, nuts, vegetables, spices, dyes, gourds, cordage, bags, bundles, baskets, and, often, bone – materials that formed the core of Maya lives and livelihoods (Dahlin et al. 2007; King 2015b: 53). Regarding nonperishable remains, the ancient Maya habitually cleaned their work areas, such that primary production debris got moved elsewhere and mixed with other kinds of junk. Thus, trash deposits indicative of production are confusingly intermingled with waste from consumption and found in secondary or tertiary contexts beyond patios and behind buildings. This makes research more time-consuming as household archaeologists must dig not just the buildings themselves but also areas beyond the buildings. On the other hand, activities inside buildings sometimes leave micro-artifacts and chemical residues, so careful sleuthing may be able to recover hints of primary production areas. Finally, since most settlements were abandoned gradually, people had time to take valuable things with them. This means that tools associated with production are often not recovered in excavations. Fortunately, rapid abandonments due to military invasion at a site like Aguateca, Guatemala, or volcanic eruption and ashfall at a site like Ceren, El Salvador, provide enticing and minimally "disturbed" snapshots of economic activity.

Specialization refers to a situation in which producers made enough of a good to be able to exchange it. As such, "fewer people make a class of objects than use it" (Costin 2001: 276). Specialization, which I gloss as crafting, does not require full-time dedication to a craft. With this definition, crafting was common among the ancient Maya. The previous section discussed one of the most important forms of specialization: intensive farming. In this section, I discuss why people chose to specialize and various details of the organization of production, including scale and the degree to which some people controlled other peoples' craftwork. I also present details of several specialized activities. These details provide a gendered portrait of production and show how the process of production entangled people of various levels of wealth and status.

In some parts of the world, people produced crafts because they did not have good land for agriculture. For example, ethnoarchaeologist Michael Deal (1998: 25) noted that twentieth-century Maya people in highland Chiapas, Mexico, turned to pottery-making because they had inadequate farmland (see also McAnany 1993). Was craftwork the province of the poor in the ancient past as well? Archaeological data show that households with evidence of craft specialization were not economically marginalized. For example, craft producers at Classic period Chunchucmil (Hutson 2010) and Colha (Potter & King 1995: 28) and Postclassic period Mayapan (Masson & Freidel 2012: 463) were wealthier than non-crafting neighbors. Often, craft specialization took place among households that also engaged in farming. Potters at Uxbenka lived among high-quality land with relatively low population density (Jordan & Prufer 2017), implying that these potters also farmed. Likewise, the first clear deposits of specialized production debris (for example, shell ornament making from Pacbitun, Belize) date to the Middle Preclassic period, when populations were low and land was abundant (Hohmann et al. 2018). Thus, relatively few households faced an "either/or" choice between farming and crafting. The motivations to engage in crafting were multiple. As markets became more common, producing for commercial exchange gave households opportunities for enrichment. Production for commercial exchange also diversified household economies, making them more resilient. Along these lines, households at Xuenkal (Ardren et al. 2016), Aguateca (Inomata 2001), and elsewhere engaged in "multi-crafting" (Hirth 2009): when a household's productive repertoire involves many specializations. Outside of market-based commercial exchange, producing a surplus and exchanging it with others helped create local and long-distance networks that bolstered social life, permitted efficiencies of scale, and could be drawn on for marriage alliances or aid during times of need. Other households produced surpluses in order to honor covenants with powerful other-than-human beings or to contribute to the fortunes of their political faction.

Other incentives for producing crafts lie at the intersection of identity and cosmology. Valuable cosmological knowledge comes to us from the Popol Vuh, an oral history of the K'iche Maya of highland Guatemala that was transcribed after Spanish contact but features stories whose elements are clearly represented in Classic period art. The Popol Vuh contains creation myths and describes two of the creators, Xpiyakok and his wife Xmukane, the oldest of the gods, as jewelers and potters, "makers and modelers" (Tedlock 1985). Xpiyakok and Xmukane's work of creation is therefore a work of crafting. Noting the parallel between creation and crafting, Reents-Budet (1994) and others have argued that the prestige of the creator gods transferred to Maya artisans. Indeed, royalty not in the line of succession could turn to vase painting, carving, and scribal arts as an honorable profession. Obviously, farmers producing pots on the side could not acquire the same cultural cachet, but in an animistic world where objects have social lives, nonroyal people's acts of making, modeling, and giving soul to clay endowed them with a culturally recognized form of dignity. The notion that crafting was an important part of the identity of non-noble people receives support from the fact that tools from a craft – masonry plastering – were found in a reverential cache at Mayapan (Masson & Peraza Lope 2014:126) and detritus from craft production has been found in caches within low-status households at Cancuen (Kovacevich 2017: 29). The identity of some crafts-people may have been durable, extending across generations (Kovacevich 2017: 24; see also Clark and Houston 1998).

Regarding the organization of production, Mayanists commonly highlight four variables roughly based on Cathy Costin's (1991) framework: where crafting took place, who was in charge, the scale of production, and the intensity of work. Among the ancient Maya, the most common values for the first two variables are that crafting took place around the house and under the control of household members. This arrangement is commonly known as household production. Looking at households on their own, the scale of crafting can range from the involvement of just a single person or multiple people. In some cases the spatial segregation of specialized production within a structure suggests that a single individual engaged in a particular craft. For example, bone needles and spindle whorls in the south room of Structure M8-10 at Aguateca (Inomata 2001) suggest a woman weaving. In other cases, the dispersion of craft residue across a domestic compound may indicate that many people in the household got involved. The largest scale of production above that of the household includes a few cases where nearly everyone in rather substantial communities specializes in the same craft. Frequently cited examples include the chert tool makers at Colha, Belize (Shafer & Hester 1983), and salt produ-cers at Salinas de los Nueve Cerros, Guatemala (Woodfill 2020). These com-munities clearly chose to specialize due to their proximity to uniquely rich natural resources: high-quality chert at Colha and the brine from an enormous inland salt dome at Salinas de los Nueve Cerros. In both cases, the quantities of goods produced far exceeded the demands of the producers; people living over 100 km from Colha acquired Colha chert tools. At a scale in between the household and the entire community, there is occasional evidence for neighbor-hood specialization (Becker 2003; Hutson 2016: 90).

Comparing Colha chert and Salinas de las Nueve Cerros salt highlights the interplay of three of the four variables: location, scale, and who is in control. The scale of chert tool production at Colha was large only in the sense that so many households participated. This large scale did not involve centralized production in something like a factory. Instead, flintknappers worked at home and, presumably, retained control of production. Thus, despite the expanded scale, chert toolmaking remains an example of household production. In contrast, salt production at Salinas de los Nueve Cerros took place at the site core in non-domestic facilities overseen by nobility. The salt workers were not their own bosses.

The disparity over who controls production invites a consideration and critique of the dichotomy between attached versus independent specialization. As traditionally defined, an attached specialist produces exclusively for, and under the watchful gaze of, a specific, powerful patron. Independent specialists produce for whomever (for an "unspecified demand," Brumfiel & Earle 1987) and they call their own shots. The ancient Maya mostly occupied a middle ground. For example, as I discuss in Section 5.1, non-noble people who undertook the first steps in the manufacture of jade adornments were clearly contracted by nobles, yet they worked at their own homes, not at someone's palace, and therefore maintained a modicum of independence regarding precisely how the work got done (what time of day, who could help, etc.). As another example, some crafters were themselves nobles who occasionally painted pots for royalty but may also have painted pots for their own purposes or to exchange with clients of similar or lower rank (Inomata 2001). Sticking with the attached/independent dichotomy would mean that at some times of day these painters were attached and at other times of the day they were independent.

In the same way that the dichotomy between attached and independent is too procrustean for the ancient Maya, the two options – full time versus part time – commonly given for the fourth variable, intensity, also constrain us unnecessarily. Most crafting among Maya households of all status levels was not full time. Rather, we find evidence of crafting in households that are also producing food (Kovacevich 2016), whether these be the workaday flintknappers at Colha or high-status multi-crafters at Aguateca (Inomata & Triadan 2000). Engaging sporadically in multiple crafts means, of course, that none can be full time. While people pursued most crafts on a part time basis, calling a specialization "part time" has the unsavory effect of implying that the artisans involved were less skilled, less dedicated, and therefore less able to meet demand. It implies that they operated in less complex economies. Hirth (2009:15) has argued that instead of focusing on the amount of time invested (something that archaeologists would have trouble quantifying precisely), we should focus on how intermittent craftwork fits with broader household strategies.

A greater understanding of the nuances of the organization of craft production best emerges by exploring the details of particular crafts. In the following section, I take a close look at the production of jade ornaments and pottery. Beyond these two crafts and the examples already given (flintknapping, salt harvesting, intensive agriculture, etc.), ancient Maya specialists made (or harvested) blades, points, and eccentric staff heads of obsidian, feathered headdresses and other garments, stones for grinding corn and other perishable goods (metates), baskets, paper, shell adornments, honey, salt, mats, and more.

5.1 Jadeworking

What we colloquially call jade can refer to two distinct minerals, jadeite and nephrite, but nephrite was not utilized by Mesoamerican lapidaries. The only known source of jadeite in Mesoamerica is in the middle Motagua Valley of Guatemala, where it occurs in the form of pebbles and boulders. While jade's rarity enhanced its value (most greenstone artifacts are in fact not jade but rather serpentine or other minerals), much of its appeal resided in its symbolic freight. The Maya equated jade with maize, fertility, water, sky, and, ultimately, ruler-ship (Taube 2005). They prized jade with deep green and blue hues, also the color of their axis mundi. Jade was undoubtedly a wealth good, as opposed to a staple good. Scholars often view wealth goods production as the province of highly skilled artisans with a mastery of esoteric knowledge and under the control of elites (Rochette 2014: 167–168). The two most detailed case studies of jadeworking uphold only parts of this view.

The first of these case studies comes from survey and excavations performed quite close to the jade source in the middle Motagua Valley. Erick Rochette (2014) found evidence for the initial stages of jade bead production at all site types in the survey area, from the smallest to the largest. Evidence for string sawing, a step in the production of earflares, was less common but also found at all site types. At sites across the Maya world, low-status households managed to acquire small quantities of jade beads (they may have served as a currency; see Section 6.3), yet earflares were affiliated almost exclusively with people of high status. Since the production of beads and earflares was dispersed well beyond the large sites where high-status people are assumed to have lived, and since the raw material was abundantly available to any resident of this valley, Rochette concludes that high-status people did not directly control jadeworking.

The second study comes from excavations by Brigitte Kovacevich (2007, 2017) at the site of Cancuen, located at the southern edge of the Lowlands, about 150 km northwest of (and across several mountain passes from) the sole source area of jade. Kovacevich recovered 3,528 pieces of greenstone debitage, weighing 77 kg, from excavations in what she refers to as commoner residential structures. Low-status households worked jade through percussion and string sawing, but there is no evidence of the final stages of production, which involve polishing and incising. Only high-status contexts contain evidence for the final stages, and these same contexts lack early stage debitage as seen in commoner residences. Thus, lower-status people completed the first production steps at home and then passed the works in progress to higher-status people for the final touches, which in some cases involved inscribing jade with text and cosmological imagery (Figure 6). These latter tasks required forms of literacy and symbolic knowledge that lower-status jade workers may have lacked. At Cancuen and many other settlements, the most prestigious jade objects, such as ear flares and masterfully incised headdress ornaments, are found only in high-status contexts such as royal and noble tombs.

The details from Cancuen suggest that jadeworking was controlled from above. Heads of powerful noble Houses likely (1) controlled the importation of raw jade from its faraway source, (2) distributed it to lesser households, who would do the more time-consuming and less-skilled labor, (3) collected the works in progress, (4) applied the finishing touches, and (5) kept the final products for themselves. Yet small beads were found among the residences that performed the first steps, suggesting to Kovacevich that these households may have been able to keep debitage that was not big enough for fashioning prestigious adornments and use it to make their own beads. These same

Figure 6 Classic period Maya carved jade ornament (K3168). Justin Kerr Maya Archive, Dumbarton Oaks, Trustees for Harvard University, Washington, DC, available under Creative Commons CC BY-SA 4.0 license, Share Alike 4.0 International.

households also had nonlocal pots (Chablekal fine grey) which they may have acquired at markets in exchange for the beads they made from scrap material. In other words, jadeworking at Cancuen was not fully controlled from above. Even if we dismiss this notion of a small bead side hustle, commoner households sawed their patrons' jade in their own homes as a kind of piecework and could control the organization of production under their own roofs.

Jadeworking was a time-consuming, strenuous process for households of modest means and those of higher standing alike. But in both cases, people at Cancuen worked jade in the same physical spaces where they spun thread for textiles, ground corn for meals, and made paper out of bark (Kovacevich 2016: 319–321). Since women participated in all three of these other activities, it is likely that women also worked jade. The people of these households were multi-crafters, intermittently engaged in various activities. The workload was high, suggesting that everyone – men, women, young, and old – pitched in.

5.2 Pottery

From an archaeological perspective, one could not find a more dramatic contrast between jade and pottery. The latter, normally found as potsherds, is usually the most common artifact, while the former is often the least common. Yet the organization of pottery production resembles jadework in some senses. For example, just as our limited data on jadeworking show household production, sometimes with minimal centralized oversight, most pottery was also made in household contexts without direct supervision. Also, people of varied status levels made pottery just as they worked jade. Furthermore, for finer pots, as with finer jades (earspools and incised pendants), the production process was segmented with different people performing different steps. Finally, there was a wide range in the quality of both jade and pottery. Given pottery's near ubiquity, I dwell on it at length, beginning with gradations in quality. Pottery, however, doesn't always dominate the archaeological record of Maya sites: An exception is rural households that used perishable container technology more often than pottery, making architectural stone the most salient artifact (Hutson & Davies 2015).

Ancient Maya pottery ran the gamut from highly prestigious to blandly perfunctory. At the high end of the spectrum we find gorgeous polychromes painted by known masters (such as T'uubul Ajaw, who painted for king Yajawte K'inich of Motul de San José, and Aj Maxam, who painted for the Kings of Naranjo) with texts that name the royal owners of the pots and imagery that includes scenes from palace life, processions, rites, mythical spectacles, flora, fauna, and more. These were often exchanged between royal courts and from royalty to nonroyalty as gifts that created and solidified alliances. These pots also served as funerary offerings, food service vessels, and records of local history and ideology. Below these are polychrome pots painted by less-skilled hands, sometimes with pseudo-glyphs: designs that look like glyphs or actual glyphs that spell only nonsense when combined. Moving toward the less prestigious end of the spectrum are bichromes and monochromes with occasional incising and other surface treatments and unslipped vessels of both medium and coarse pastes.

Given the boisterous variation in the finished products, we can expect a carnival parade of production situations. Unfortunately, Mayanists have struggled to reconstruct the social and technical organization of pottery making because they have found so few contexts of production. The culprit here is the practice of firing pots in the open without a kiln (potential kilns have been reported only at a few sites in Belize [Lopez Varela et al. 1999; Masson 2000: 81–87] and western Honduras [Schortman et al. 2001]). Unlike kiln firing, open firing leaves no architectural traces. Furthermore, firing temperatures are usually not hot enough to produce warped and/or blistered wasters. Polychromes and other fine vessels that need firing temperatures high enough to produce wasters can be placed inside other vessels – saggars – as part of an open fire. In the absence of workshops, archaeologists have relied on less direct evidence, which is often scant. Nevertheless, several lines of evidence have been used to identify potting locales. The four examples of potting locations I present later in this section (Tikal, Uxbenka, Motul de San Jose, and Buenavista) highlight the range in forms of evidence.

The first is residential group 4H-1 at Tikal, located about 1 km east of the site core. Years after the 1962 excavations, Becker (2003) argued for polychrome production based on the presence a relatively large number of molds and a deposit of polychrome sherds that is too big (1 m high and 75 m^3) to result from polychrome consumption and more likely resulted from decades of dumping shattered, misfired pots (about a quarter of the pots in open firings crack or otherwise turn out badly). Group 4H-1 is at the edge a of natural depression (a bajo) with excellent clay for potting. At Uxbenka, Belize, Jordan and Prufer (2017) identify three potting locales based on the presence of tools for "smoothing, scraping, incising, polishing, and boring." All three locales also had unusually high quantities of particular ceramic types, which, according to Stark (2007), indicates production of that type. Like Group 4H-1, the Uxbenka potting locales were located on the periphery of the site. At Motul de San José, Guatemala, Halperin and Foias (2012) found by-products of polychrome pottery in a midden at the site's central Acropolis. The most salient evidence includes (1) wasters in the form of bubbly, vitrified, spalled, twisted, and/or warped sherds; (2) carbon flakes, grey ash, and burnt clay lumps potentially removed from the firing location; (3) paint pots with residues of red pigment and bone pins with the same pigments on their tips; (4) polishers and smoothers; and (5) figurine molds and duplicates.

Research by Reents-Budet and colleagues (Reents-Budet et al. 2000) that combines chemical composition through instrumental neutron activation analysis, artifact provenience, and analysis of vessel form, iconography, and texts has detected the existence of workshops in the eastern Peten and western Belize. Potsherds with similar paste recipes (indicated by compositional groups) also share the same painting styles and vessel forms and tend to be most common at a particular site, such as Buneavista del Cayo, Belize. Reents-Budet and colleagues assume that the workshop was located in the Buenavista palace since a deposit of secondary refuse associated with the palace contained paint pots and potting tools. One of the interesting results of the chemical composition studies of pottery at Buenavista was that widely available day-to-day service wares, including monochromes and unslipped pots, are linked chemically to the special purpose polychromes, indicating that the same workshops were producing pottery of high, medium, and low prestige. Likewise, Triadan and Inomata (2020) argue that "elites" at Aguateca made their own undecorated storage jars.

These data about the location of pottery production contribute to the discussion of the organization of production. It is already clear that the location of production of both prestigious and less prestigious pottery varied from site to site. For example, polychromes were made at the Motul de San José and Buenavista site cores, but on the periphery of Tikal's settlement. Likewise, if the Buenavista workshop, which produced both polychromes and everyday pottery, was indeed located in the palace, then in the case of Buenavista (and perhaps Aguateca), everyday pottery was made at site cores and in the peripheries, while in other cases (Uxbenka, Palenque, Tikal) it was made well outside of the site core.

The phrases "palace school" and "palace workshop" have been used to describe pottery-making at Buenavista and Motul de San José, yet since production debris comes from secondary contexts, we don't know if production within the palaces took place in homes or non-domestic workshops. Clearly, some of this work is attached since some pots were commissioned by royalty. Production was segmented in the sense that the people who painted polychromes are probably not the ones who prepared the clay and shaped the vessels (Halperin & Foias 2012). Looking at painting alone, Coggins (1975) suggested that in some cases more than one person was involved in painting a single pot. Yet the co-occurrence of shaping tools and painting tools in the same dumps at the Buenavista and Motul de San José site cores suggests both tasks were performed nearby.

Potting outside of site cores, which accounts for most of the pots used in the past, would be considered household production. Household production of less prestigious pottery was most likely segmented as well. Mesoamerican ethnographies contain many examples in which different people work on different aspects of pot-making. For example, in Santa Maria Chiquimula, Guatemala, men form the vessels, women fire them, and women and children prepare clay, add handles, and burnish vessel surfaces (Reina & Hill 1978: 70). Callaghan's (2016) survey of ethnographic literature shows that the Chiquimula example is somewhat unusual because potting, while open to both men and women in some communities, is in fact a female activity in most Maya communities. At the time of conquest, Yucatec terms for potting in the Northern Maya Lowlands suggest that men shaped vessels though it is likely that women also participated in production (Clark & Houston 1998; Callaghan 2016). Most scholars believe that in the Classic period, women played a major role, and in many cases the main role, in making pots (Callaghan 2016). Joyce (1993) notes that several steps in pottery-making have direct analogs in an activity known to be closely linked with women: food preparation. Preparing paste (griding and mixing materials) parallels the preparation of food ingredients, shaping vessels parallels shaping tamales, and firing pots parallels cooking food.

Several lines of evidence suggest people did not make pots full time. To begin with, moisture during the monsoon-like wet season probably prevented proper drying and firing conditions from about June to October. Also, many potters were multi-crafters (Callaghan & Kovacevich 2020). Since multi-crafters practiced a variety of crafts, they did not commit full time to a single one. Measurements of standardization in the production of utilitarian pottery suggest relatively low degrees of intensity, a situation in which many people made pots intermittently as opposed to a few people making pots all the time.

6 Exchange

What we saw in the previous section – many households specialized in order to produce surplus – brings up the question of what they did with this surplus. Households likely exchanged some portion of their surplus to acquire goods that they did not produce themselves. Political and religious leaders likely collected tribute or tax, and households either rendered a portion of their surplus to these leaders or traded their surplus to get the kinds of goods leaders expected as payment. Either way, most ancient Maya households were not self-sufficient. Few if any households gathered, on their own, all the raw materials they required nor fabricated all the finished goods they needed. Instead, exchange was a critical factor in provisioning Maya society and enriching social life. Many different forms of exchange took place in ancient Maya societies, including balanced reciprocity, redistribution, gift exchange, and more. Several recent studies make the case that marketplace exchange accompanied these other forms of exchange. This section discusses these forms of exchange with particular attention to markets. In reference to markets, I will cover a variety of questions, such as the following: What is marketplace exchange? Why were marketplace studies slow to enter the mainstream of Maya research? How do Mayanists claim to detect marketplace exchange? What was the geographic reach of markets? Who controlled and/or benefitted from them? And, finally, did the Maya have money?

Balanced reciprocity is when one household attains a good from another (usually a neighboring household or one that contains kin or friends) and will pay them back, but not immediately. Normally, the exact worth of the good is not negotiated so the payback is only roughly equivalent in value and takes the form of a different kind of good. As Aristotle speculated over two millennia ago, different households specialized in different things and shared them informally. Sheets (2000) argues that the households of Cerén, El Salvador, were engaged in balanced reciprocity, though he calls this "horizontal economy" or "village economy." Specifically, each of the three households that were extensively excavated produced items to exchange with neighbors. Household 1 produced surplus thread, hammerstones, and grinding stones. Household 2 produced decorated gourds. Household 4 grew abundant agave and mirasol, which allowed them to supply the other households in the village with fibers and poles for construction. Occasionally, archaeologists refer to balanced reciprocity as barter (see see Section 6.3 for more comments on barter).

Redistribution is when centralized authorities collect various resources – let's use cotton and honey as examples – from subject households in the form of tax or tribute and then dole out a portion of these resources to the households from which they were collected (cotton to those who initially contributed honey, and honey to those who initially contributed cotton). The authorities usually keep a share of the resources for themselves and use another share strategically to create or strengthen alliances with powerful actors. Redistribution implies a high degree of centralized management of the economy as leaders oversee collection, storage, and dissemination of both staples and wealth goods. Since Maya city state capitals lacked extensive storehouses such as those seen, for example, at Inca administrative centers, they were probably not collecting and redistributing significant amounts of bulk goods. At the site of Copan, Aoyama (2001: 351) argues that "possible political control over [obsidian] blade allocation can be inferred from the skewed distribution of these artifacts." Specifically, at the beginning of the Classic period, the inhabitants of the principal group at Copan appear to be the only people making obsidian blades and the larger, higher-status households at the site acquire more blades than everyone else. In the Late Classic period, blade production was no longer restricted to the site core and nearly everyone living in the site had access to obsidian, yet rural households had less access. Aoyama (2001: 355) acknowledges that differential access to obsidian "could have partly resulted from the greater purchasing power of the households involved" but he believes instead that the pattern supports the existence of centralized redistribution.

Feasts can also count as redistribution. Dietler and Hayden (2001: 65) define feasts as "ritual activity that involves the communal consumption of food and drink." There are many kinds of feasts. Among the ancient Maya, the inclusionary feast is an excellent form of redistribution in that a patron, usually in a position of authority and not a food producer, acquires "abundant amounts of commonly consumed food" from supporters and serves it to large groups of people in order to gain solidarity and build trust (Lecount 2001: 935; see also Golden & Scherer 2013; Masson & Peraza Lope 2014). Inclusionary feasts are a common form of rewarding laborers on monumental building projects but can also take place on a smaller scale to strengthen bonds of community, as Yaeger (2000) argues for the San Lorenzo nieghborhood at Xunantunich.

While it is clear that the distribution of some goods (for example, the jade earspools mentioned in the production section) was clearly under control by leaders, the lack of major storage facilities and the comparatively underdeveloped bureaucracies in Maya city-states suggest that redistribution was a relatively minor form of exchange among the ancient Maya (Masson & Freidel 2012: 457). To quote Stark and Garraty (2010: 44):

> It is unlikely that ancient states or imperial powers invested in regular household provisioning of quotidian items or possessed the logistical capabilities for such large-scale dissemination. Ancient states busied themselves with a considerable agenda of political, ritual, and class-related goals, with challenges to assure sufficient revenues; provisioning of quotidian goods would not have contributed to any of these objectives and, in fact, would have been exceptionally costly.

Indeed, Timothy Earle (1977) has shown that in Contact era Hawai'i, which was once the poster child case study of redistribution, chiefs in fact redistributed very few of the resources they extracted from clients. Instead, they used them for their own purposes and left local communities to fend for themselves. While Rice (1987: 77) agrees that high-level officials at Classic period Maya centers did not administer the redistribution of basic goods, she argues that low-level redistributive networks may have existed among kin groups. In this scenario, small groups of producers give their wares to the kin group head who would then redistribute them among the groups.

Gift-giving is another form of exchange, detected most easily with luxury goods such as polychrome pottery with texts. One of the best examples is a vase recovered from the tomb of a prince at Buenavista, a small political center in Belize (Taschek & Ball 1989). This tall, cylindrical pot, named the Jauncy vase, features extremely elegant paintings of the dancing maize god (Figure 7). The text around the rim identifies it as the chocolate drinking vase of king K'ak Tiliw Chan Chak, who ruled the major site of Naranjo, 17 km west of Buenavista, from 693 CE to about 728 CE. Buenavista was most likely a subordinate ally of Naranjo and K'ak Tiliw actively cultivated this alliance by giving gifts. Many other examples exist; households at El Perú/Waká, located in the western Peten, received pots from the rulers of polities to the east such as Motul de San José and El Zotz (Eppich & Freidel 2015). While the Jauncy vase is a masterpiece of Maya pottery, LeCount (1999) has argued that political operators gave fine but

Figure 7 The Jauncy vase, excavated from Buenavista del Cayo, Belize (K4464). Justin Kerr Maya Archive, Dumbarton Oaks, Trustees for Harvard University, Washington, DC, available under Creative Commons CC BY-SA 4.0 license, Share Alike 4.0 International.

much less remarkable serving vessels as gifts to clients of much lower social standing as a way of building vertical alliances. Such decorated pottery can therefore serve as a form of political currency as opposed to an indicator of social status. On the other hand, certain kinds of polychrome at Tikal were broadly distributed, potentially indicating market exchange (Masson 2020; see Section 6.2).

Long-distance exchange was prominent. The Maya Lowlands lack obsidian sources and therefore its residents imported volcanic glass from Highland Guatemala and Central Mexico. In most cases, obsidian traveled 200 km or more from its source and up to 600 km as the crow flies for sites in the Northern Lowlands. Excavations show that households of all social status levels had access to obsidian. I discuss potential geopolitical disruptions to long-distance trade further below, but in short it seems clear that, at certain times, some long-distance trade was not monopolized by royal families and traders could operate independently of political boundaries. At other times, such as the Early Postclassic, state agents at Chichén Itzá were clearly managing the import of obsidian from sources in Central Mexico located well over 1,000 km away, such as Ucareo, Pachuca, Paredón, and Zaragoza (Braswell & Glasscock 2002). This would also have been the case for pottery made at Teotihuacan and placed in the Copan tombs (a distance of about 1,500 km) of dynastic founder Yax K'uk' Mo' and his wife. Perishable goods traded over hundreds of kilometers include bird feathers, salt, cacao, and more

"Market exchange" as discussed by economists refers to transactions in which the forces of supply and demand have a major effect on prices (Garraty 2010). Market exchange, however, is always institutionalized, which means that it always takes place within a social context that affects pricing. In other words, supply and demand do not exclusively determine price. Other factors might intervene, such as social relations between buyer and seller and the influence of guilds or governments. Since it is difficult to imagine market exchange taking place in the absence of a social context, variables beyond supply and demand always affect prices. A marketplace is a physical space where multiple buyers and sellers congregate to exchange a variety of goods. Market exchange can occur outside of marketplaces in the case of itinerant peddlers or transactions at the point of production. In reality, Mayanists do not have sufficient evidence to determine the degree to which supply and demand affected prices. In the absence of specific data on supply and demand, Mayanists tacitly use a different definition of market exchange that is best understood in terms of how it differs from reciprocity and redistribution. In contrast to redistribution, where households may have no choice regarding the kind or quantity of goods that leaders allot them, marketplace exchange presumes that consumers have a choice of what, and how much, to purchase. They enter transactions willingly even if one might perceive a lack of equivalence in the value of the items being exchanged. In contrast to reciprocity, in which the receiver need not immediately offer something in return, in market-based commerce, the parties to the exchange complete the transaction in a single moment during which each side hands over to the other the items they agree to swap. In those cases where the swap is not simultaneous, debts or tabs might accrue but these differ from the kinds of belated obligations characteristic of balanced reciprocity in that the amount owed is exact. Regrettably, Mayanists can't actually muster evidence to demonstrate these conditions.

Thus, in the absence of data on a primary force that affects price (supply and demand) or the precise conditions surrounding market exchange (voluntary transactions in which both sides normally exchange goods at the same moment), Mayanists fall back on other proxies for market exchange. For the Postclassic period, Spanish documents about the existence of marketplaces are not particularly robust (see Section 6.1), but they at least made it safe to assume some degree of marketing took place. Ethnohistorical records mention large markets near the coast in northeastern Yucatan and others in the interior. They also mention professional traveling merchants called *p'olom* (King 2020). Documents from the Maya Highlands suggest that a majority of households depended on marketplaces for everyday needs (King 2015b:38). Archaeologists studying the Postclassic period have substantiated these historical sources by documenting a rise in obsidian exchange, the appearance of bustling centers on coastal trade routes, and changes in ceramic production geared toward exports (Sabloff & Rathje 1975; Masson & Peraza Lope 2014: 26). For the Classic period, however, several conditions discouraged research on markets. Therefore, archaeological proxies for Classic period marketplaces were slow to develop. Before exploring these proxies, I begin by discussing why it took so long for a critical mass of archaeologists to take seriously the possibility of markets in the Classic period.

6.1 What Held Back Studies of Classic Period Markets?

Mayanists were slow to entertain the possibility of marketplaces for a number of reasons. First, in the middle of the twentieth century, Karl Polanyi, whose writings on traditional economies resonated with a generation of anthropologists, made the notion of pre-modern markets unpalatable. He saw market exchange as implying a rational maximization mindset favored by Adam Smith. Polanyi (1944) thought that in small societies with strong webs of kinship and social solidarity, a market mentality would threaten community well-being. In other words, rational maximizing supposedly led to ruthless haggling and the search for individual gain at others' expense, which in turn led to the kind of hostility and antagonism that, far from advancing the interests of the community as a whole, would tear it apart. Thus, markets should only exist in contexts where powerful authorities regulate prices. Polanyi concluded that the dominant mode of exchange in village societies was reciprocity and the dominant mode of exchange in chiefdoms was redistribution. Markets only dominated in modern states.

Polanyi is probably best remembered for his insistence that exchange is always embedded in institutions (see Section 3). Polanyi's core idea of embeddedness appeals to anthropologists because we are committed to the recognition of cultural diversity and the assertion that universal claims about human nature, such as Adam Smith's market mentality, are in fact culturally specific. Yet the entirely tenable idea of the embeddedness of pre-modern economies entailed the non-tenable position that pre-modern people simply couldn't think rationally.

While this Element is not the place to pick apart the prominence of *Homo economicus* in contemporary economies, it is worth exploring a more realistic picture of pre-modern actors. Blanton and Fargher (2010) detect in Polanyi's writings an idealization of pre-modern communities reminiscent of the "herd mentality" of villagers described in Marx's Asiatic mode of production. The occupants of these communities were said to be mired in customs and values that provided easy opportunities for exploitative despots. Such villagers lacked a sense of private enterprise and therefore refused to produce more than what was necessary for subsistence, communal ritual, or elite extraction. In short, Blanton and Fargher charge that ancient people in Polanyi's model were not agents: They could recognize neither exploitation nor opportunity and therefore could not act strategically in response to either. Political texts from the Classic period reveal Maya lords to be cunning and agentive, even if their actions were structured by tradition (as is the case with actors everywhere). If royal households could scheme, so too could humble households, even if the resources that underwrote calculative action were more modest.

A second reason for the slow development of studies of marketing among the ancient Maya was the dearth of documentary evidence. Archaeologists in Central Mexico (Berdan 1983; Blanton 1985; Hodge & Minc 1990) benefit from a large body of eyewitness accounts, dating from the arrival of the Spaniards 500 years ago, of the existence of what Europeans referred to as marketplaces. In the Maya area, the ethnohistorical evidence is not as strong. When the Spaniards established a colony in Northern Yucatan in the 1540s, European diseases had already drastically lowered local populations.

Furthermore, local political and economic organizations had been deeply disrupted by the fragmentation of the Mayapan confederacy in the fifteenth century and a variety of droughts and famines (Masson & Freidel 2013). Thus, conquest-era Maya marketplaces and marketing were not as developed as those in Central Mexico.

Furthermore, the rich Classic period corpus of texts and art is mostly silent on economics, much less marketplaces. This lacuna encourages a perspective that ancient Maya economies may not have been very complex (Chase et al. 2015: 227–8). As noted in Section 6, occasional finds like the Buenavista vase attest to gift-giving, but only give voice to high-level schemes and networks of patronage. Since nobles are the only agents in the textual record, this record remains silent on the possibility that non-nobles could act with just as much guile. Palace scenes painted on polychrome pots and murals show the presentation of tribute, sometimes quantified, as in the bundles of 8,000 cacao beans depicted in a throne room in the Bonampak murals. Yet tribute presentation again directs us away from commerce. Merchants rarely, if ever, appear in palace scenes. This scarcity signifies not the absence of merchants but rather their lower status (McAnany 2010: 256; Masson & Freidel 2013: 209; Tokovinine & Beliaev 2013: 172). The often adversarial nature of interactions between the Classic period god of merchants, God L, and the divine patrons of royalty, such as the sun god, the maize god, and the hero twins, reflects "ambivalence in the classic Maya attitude toward trade and traders" (Tokovinine & Beliaev 2013:174).

A remarkable set of murals from the Chiik Nahb acropolis at Calakmul (Carrasco Vargas et al. 2009) depicts, in the eyes of most researchers, scenes of men and women engaging in commercial exchange (Figure 8). Calakmul was an enormous and geopolitically dominant capital in the central Lowlands of Campeche, Mexico. Appropriately, these murals come from a location whose architectural traits actually suggest the presence of a marketplace (see Section 6.2). Yet these murals were discovered relatively recently. Other iconographic hints about commerce, including representations of God L and depictions at Chichen Itza of travelers with bundles, argued to represent merchants (Tokovinine & Beliaev 2013), do not unequivocally represent marketplace exchange.

A third reason for the slow development of market studies is that researchers had to disabuse themselves of strongly voiced but misleading perspectives within the field of Maya archaeology surrounding ecology, demography, and the importance of non-nobles. Archaeologists have often thought that markets appear in contexts with high environmental diversity and high population density. Initially the Maya were thought to lack both of these, thus making markets seem improbable. Furthermore, too much focus on leaders and not

Figure 8 Chiik Nahb mural, Calakmul, Mexico, available under Creative commons, Share Alike 2.0: https://creativecommons.org/licenses/by-sa/2.0/deed.en.

enough focus on people of lower status have also slowed consideration of markets. I now expand on each of these three causes – misunderstanding of ecology, underestimation of population density, and lack of focus on lower-status people – for the delay in thinking about ancient Maya markets, beginning with ecology (see also King & Shaw 2015).

In an area with high environmental diversity, communities located relatively close to each other may each control a unique environmental resource. Assuming that each community desires access to the resources controlled exclusively by other communities, a marketplace that makes each of these resources available serves the interests of all communities. At the same time, one could argue that high environmental diversity lends itself not to a market, but to the evolution of powerful centralized authorities that serve to control the distribution of the resources from each patch in the mosaic (e.g. Sanders 1977). Regardless of the mechanism of exchange (markets versus redistribution) responsible for circulating goods in such a context, Sanders and Price (1968) argued that the Maya Lowlands did not exhibit significant environmental diversity. The Maya Lowlands were instead thought to be characterized by resource redundancy. However, several studies have shown that resources in the Maya Lowlands are not as evenly dispersed as once thought (Fedick 1996; Gomez-Pompa et al. 2003). Lowland resources such as salt, chert, and cacao are famously patchy. But even in areas without such assets, other features such as escarpments, swamp edges, karst depressions, rivers, and fracture zones each permit local resource specializations. Such resource diversity and community specialization have fueled market-based models of ancient

Maya economies: "By combining the variety and abundance of specialized production at a marketplace ... a greater region of communities obtained the necessary balance of resources for a sustainable harvesting of an otherwise fragile environment" (Scarborough & Valdez 2009: 211).

Regarding population density, it was once thought that major Maya sites were vacant ceremonial centers (Willey & Bullard 1965) or that they were regal-ritual centers (Sanders & Webster 1988) containing little more than the locus of royal ceremonies and the extended family of the king and his servants. In both models, the ancient Maya lack high population density. High population density encourages markets for two reasons. First, in urban contexts with high population density, farmland is distant and presumably not all residents are farmers: some are administrators, craft specialists, and nobles. Though some of these actors may get food via tribute, a marketplace would help provision the others. Alternatively, tribute that is not edible can be exchanged for food at marketplaces (Brumfiel 1980). Second, it becomes more cost-effective for someone to sell goods when many consumers live nearby (Blanton & Fargher 2010; Hirth 2010). If consumers do not live near sellers, the cost of transporting goods to consumers reduces the sellers' profitability. On the other side of the coin, if vendors are not itinerant, the cost to consumers of traveling to multiple different vendors for household needs is prohibitive, thus encouraging less production for trade and more self-sufficiency and reciprocity. Though markets thrive in areas with high settlement density, this does not mean that they would tank in areas of low settlement density. David Freidel (1981) argues that when rural Maya people make pilgrimages to attend ceremonies at larger settlements, markets spring up to serve them. Freidel's ideas go some distance in explaining how centers with enormous plazas and pyramids, the ceremonial pageantry performed therein, and pop-up markets on the side, could pull in dispersed rural farmers and integrate Maya societies and economies.

Did ancient Maya cities have high settlement densities? Maya cities were generally much less densely populated than old world cities. The average density of a sample of 600 old world cities is close to 13,000 people per km^2 (Storey 2006). Mesoamerica's most densely populated city – Teotihuacan – held barely 6,000 people per km^2. The most densely populated Classic period Maya cities (Palenque, Chunchucmil, and Dzibilchaltun) range between about 2,000 and 3,500 people per km^2 (Hutson 2016). Most Maya cities had fewer than 1,000 people per km^2. Yet the precise density of Maya cities may not be as important as their high populations. In the 1960s, the publication of maps of Tikal, Mayapan, and Dzibilchaltun, which showed thousands of domestic compounds clustered around site cores, fueled "a growing consensus that the great lowland Maya centers were considerably more like true cities than some of the opponents of this idea had originally supposed" (Ashmore & Willey 1981: 16).

The acceptance of the idea that the ancient Maya had large cities with tens of thousands of inhabitants did not lead directly to a consideration of markets. Instead, attention shifted to discussions of the kinds of agricultural intensification that could have supported these populations. Amidst this focus on food production, most scholars assumed that redistribution channeled crops from intensive fields to hungry mouths. While scholars writing about cities in other parts of the world considered the marketplace as a primary means of supplying calories (Brumfiel 1980; Alston 1998), hardly anyone considered the possibility that markets played a role in distributing food among the Maya (Dahlin et al. 2010: 193).

Regarding a lack of focus on non-nobles, approaches that pay more attention to high-status people are less likely to consider market exchange than approaches that also consider the livelihoods of households that farm, fish, and engage in the production of everyday goods. The upper classes have much to gain from markets, as I discuss in Section 7, but Maya archaeologists' traditional preoccupation with palaces, temples, and hieroglyphic inscriptions often led to consideration of themes such as alliance building, ritual practice, and legitimation of authority. In the last forty years, the growth of household archaeology and the acknowledgment that the hoi polloi, just like the high and mighty, act strategically and with agency (Lohse & Valdez 2004; Robin 2013) has broadened consideration of markets. Specifically, markets provide benefits to common households. They don't just make exchange more efficient, they also encourage crafting by providing a venue for selling different sorts of surplus products, therefore allowing the diversification of household economies (Sheets 2000; Hirth 2010). The goal of such diversifications is not just to get by, but to create wealth for their own social and political initiatives.

Despite these barriers to research on Classic period markets, several authors in the 1980s and 1990s considered the possibility. David Freidel (1981) argued that when massive ceremonies and rituals drew rural settlers to religious centers, marketplaces most likely accompanied these events. To support this position, Freidel referred to the conjunction of markets and religious events in Medieval Europe and historic and contemporary Guatemala. Though Freidel's argument did not refer to any particular archaeological site, other authors writing at about the same time as Freidel proposed that specific plazas at specific sites, such as Tikal, Sayil, Coba, and Ceibal, served as marketplaces (Shaw 2012). Yet these proposals from thirty years ago did not gain much traction because of a shortage of research specifically designed to test the existence of marketplace commerce.

6.2 Evidence for Market Exchange among the Classic Period Maya

The shortage of research grew largely from a lack of methods for identifying markets. In 1998, however, Ken Hirth published an article describing three approaches – configurational, contextual, and distributional – that Mayanists have subsequently embraced in the search for ancient commerce. Each of these approaches entails a set of expectations that can be tested using evidence from the archaeological record. At the site of Chunchucmil, located at the northwest tip of the Yucatan Peninsula, Bruce Dahlin and colleagues explicitly devised a research design to test all three approaches, so I use Chunchucmil as the key example while also referring to other sites.

The configurational approach focuses on locating the actual physical spaces that served as marketplaces. Marketing as defined in Section 6 does not require a dedicated space, so an inability to find one does not put marketing out of the question. Such spaces should be easily accessible, should be able to accommodate lots of people, may have residues of trade and exchange, and may have rows of market stalls. At Chunchucmil, Dahlin and colleagues (2007) presented multiple lines of evidence to support the argument that Plaza D was a marketplace (Figure 9). The plaza is located in the exact center of the city, at the confluence of several causeways. Furthermore, no architectural features restrict access to the plaza. Thus, it is easy to get to and easy to enter. While the plaza has a small temple, similar to Aztec marketplaces, it lacks the kinds of large temples that mark other plazas as dedicated primarily to ritual and political pageantry. Excavations revealed rock alignments that could have served as footing for rows of market stalls. Soil chemical analysis revealed a band of very high phosphate readings aligned with the purported stalls. Based on soil chemistry analysis of contemporary marketplaces in the Maya area, the high phosphate readings likely indicate food service areas of a market. There was no evidence of feasting in Plaza D. Chemical testing of other plazas at Chunchucmil failed to identify traces of marketplaces.

The Chiik Nahb Complex at Calakmul is also an excellent candidate for a marketplace. As already mentioned, it has murals that depict scenes of men and women giving, receiving, and consuming a variety of goods (Figure 8). Hieroglyphs close to each person read as labels – "tamale person," "maize gruel person," "clay vessel person," "salt person," and "tobacco person" (Carrasco Vargas et al. 2009; Martin 2012). Situated within the Calakmul site core, on the north side of the plaza that contains the site's largest building (Str. II) and its palace (Str. III), the Chiik Nahb complex is a 2.5 ha space containing sixty-eight buildings, most of which sit low to the ground, organized in rows running north/south. Folan and colleagues (2001: 234) suggest that this complex may be

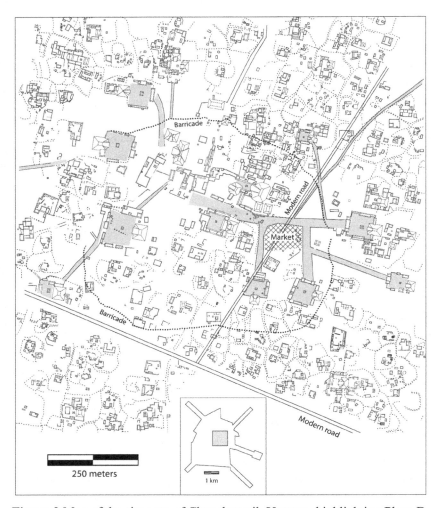

Figure 9 Map of the site core of Chunchucmil, Yucatan, highlighting Plaza D, the marketplace.

a marketplace: The rows of low structures could be market stalls. Chris Jones long argued that the galleries east of the ballcourt in the East Plaza at Tikal comprised a marketplace.

The distributional approach focuses on how the existence of a marketplace affects household provisioning (Hirth 1998). This approach assumes that if a particular good is available at a marketplace, it should have a broad, relatively homogeneous distribution. As long as most households have the means to purchase the good and the desire to acquire it, archaeologists should find that good distributed more or less evenly across the different areas of a site and among households of different levels of wealth and/or power. Alternatively, in redistribution, elites control access to a good, keep a lot of that good for themselves and their cronies, and pass only a small portion to humble households that have given them loyalty, labor, or surplus goods. Thus, distribution will be skewed strongly toward elites. Economies known to feature marketplaces according to historical documents do indeed show the widespread access to goods predicted by the distributional approach (Greene 1986).

At Chunchucmil, my colleagues and I amassed viable excavation data from 130 of the 1,447 different architectural compounds mapped at the site (Hutson 2017). We selected these 130 compounds in order to create a sample that was representative in terms of location across the site as well as the wealth level of the ancient occupants. We found that there is almost no difference in access to obsidian and luxury pottery among richer and poorer households. There is also no difference in access from one part of the site to another. These results suggest that Chunchucmil's households had open access to obsidian and fine pottery at the central marketplace: Plaza D. Other archaeologists have deployed the distributional approach at sites such as El Perú/Waká (Eppich & Freidel 2015) and Chichen Itza (Braswell & Glascock 2002) though sampling has not been representative.

The contextual approach focuses on features that one would normally expect to find in a market economy, features that greatly facilitate marketing, and/or features that demand the presence of a market (Hrith 1998: 453). Examples of such features include large cities, craft specialization, location near a trade route, transportation infrastructure that supports trade, and more. Chunchucmil was located near a vigorous maritime trade route along the coast of the Gulf of Mexico and had a port site – Canbalam – on this route. Chunchucmil was a large city (over 30,000 people during its peak at the end of the Early Classic period) with a high population density (over 3,000 people per km^2 in its central 6 km^2). As already discussed, large cities are conducive to markets because large populations equate to high demand for goods and high population density cuts down on travel time for vendors and consumers, making exchange more efficient. Furthermore, Chunchucmil's hinterland contained dozens of villages and towns. The land in and around Chunchucmil was not sufficient to meet the food needs of both the city center and its outlying settlement, in part because Chunchucmil was located near the edge of the seasonally inundated Savannah that grades westward toward estuary and the Gulf of Mexico. Excavations in domestic compounds tested the expectation that Chunchucmil's households engaged in craft specialization. Based on nonperishable artifacts, we located households that specialized in the processing of fibers, the production of marine shell ornaments, and activities dedicated to grinding. While the nonperishable data for specialization is not overwhelming, Dahlin and others (2017) make a compelling argument that Chunchucmil was located in such a way as to enable specialization in a variety of perishable resources. Chief among these is salt. Mesoamerica's second largest saltworks lie 27 km northwest of Chunchucmil, adjacent to its port, and scholars have long been aware of extensive Contact-era trade in salt (Andrews 1983). The coast would also have supplied marine fauna. Savannah resources include logwood dye, cordage, roofing thatch, wild game, and favorable conditions for apiculture.

Caracol, Belize, provides another example of the contextual approach (Chase et al. 2015). It was located on a trade route, enhanced by causeways, that connected resources from the Maya mountains (to the east) to population centers in the southern Peten (to the west). It was an extraordinarily large city in the Late Classic; estimates of about 100,000 inhabitants, recently substantiated by lidar data, make it the most highly populated of all Maya cities. Though population density was low (about 600 people per km^2), the city featured the Maya area's most extensive network of causeways. This network helps vendors and consumers get to markets, many of which were located on plazas attached to the causeways. Excavations in 150 residential compounds show specialized production (lithics, shell, cloth, bone, and woodworking) in most of these compounds. Likewise, these households acquired several goods from far away, such as obsidian, Belize Red pottery, and jadeite.

More recently, linguistic evidence has bolstered Classic period archaeological evidence. Tokovinine and Beliaev (2013) note that native cognate words for buying (*man*), selling (*chon*), bartering (*k'ex*), trading/profiting (*p'ol*), and market (*k'iwik*, which can also mean plaza) are found in Maya languages known to have split from each other by the end of the first Millennium BCE. This means that "market exchange played a significant role in Classic Maya society, with all the essential terms for trade-related activities already in place by the first millennium CE" (Tokovinine and Beliaev 2013: 172). In a parallel yet independent study, Speal (2014: 105, 107) concludes "that there was a complex of cognate words relating selling activity to patios, platforms, or plazas ... around the middle of the Late Formative period" and that "the florescence of commercial terminology, if not the initial appearance of 'commerce' itself, in Mayan languages" dates to between 1100 and 800 BCE.

Regarding the chronological origin of marketplaces, Tokovinine and Beliaev (2013: 172) state that "linguistic data suggest that key market-related activities in the Maya Lowlands emerged in the Preclassic period" (see also Speal 2014; Freidel & Reilly 2010). Furthermore, several authors have documented voluminous long-distance exchange of obsidian in the Preclassic. Indeed, production for exchange is a common household strategy with early origins in many parts of the world, though evidence for exchange does not necessarily imply markets. An explicit deployment of the distributional approach in the search for Preclassic market activity at the site of Ucí and its neighbors (Hutson 2021) showed that pottery and perhaps a few perishable goods were exchanged according to market principles (possibly in the absence of an actual market-place) but most goods were exchanged in other ways. I argued that the discordant lines of evidence indicate a grey area at the very beginning of market exchange. At Ucí, the rise of political integration as seen in the construction of an inter-site causeway implies the creation of an institutional framework that could provide the kind of stability necessary for an incipient market. This pattern – incipient market exchange coinciding with increased political centralization – follows Graeber's (2011) argument that politics and the origins of markets are closely intertwined.

Another important question surrounding markets is the size of the area they serviced. We don't have much data on this (cf. Eppich & Freidel 2015: 218). The reach of the Motul de San Jose market perhaps extended 32 km beyond the city (Halperin et al. 2009). Chunchucmil's market did not serve its hinterland very well, suggesting a much smaller radius. Smaller radii are also proposed for marketplaces in Postclassic Central Mexico but here city state capitals themselves were packed in more closely. Obviously, exotic long-distance goods (jade, obsidian) traveled far beyond the radius of any particular market, and in Section 7 I discuss the issue of the effect of geopolitical relations on the passage of these items. But what about bulk goods? Along navigable rivers and the coast, bulk goods were moved efficiently in long, dugout canoes in both the Classic and Postclassic periods. Traveling overland, the Maya had neither beasts of burden nor wheeled transport, a stark difference from pre-modern economies in the Old World. Yet with tumplines and backracks, human porters could carry upwards of 50 kg. A number of studies show that in Mesoamerica, distances of between 50 and 100 km are entirely feasible in terms of costs and benefits for transporting bulk foods by foot. These distances cross Maya city state boundaries and likely also extend beyond the radii of market service areas. As Masson and Freidel note (2012: 477, 2013: 219), food interdependency among regions separated by such distances was probably very common among the ancient Maya. From year to year, rainfall can be well above or below the annual average, and even when enough rain falls, it may fall at the wrong time of year. Thus, localized failed harvests drove a need for bulk food exchange (Freidel & Shaw 2000; Masson & Peraza Lope 2014: 274). But food interdependency resulted not just from fluctuations in agricultural productivity. In some places, bulk exchange occurred simply because densely populated areas couldn't produce enough food (Canuto et al. 2018; Hutson 2017; Hutson et al. 2021a). Corn could be stored for up to three years and leaders amassed currencies such as shell beads to trade for corn (Freidel & Shaw 2000). Marketplaces in Mesoamerica played a key role here because they "had an enormous effect in mobilizing bulk resources over short to intermediate distances of 30 to 150 km" (Hirth & Pillsbury 2013: 15; Tokovinine and Beliaev 2013:170).

To summarize, how widespread was market exchange? Clearly, marketing took place at several ancient Maya cities, but it remains difficult to assess the prevalence of marketing in comparison to other forms of exchange taking place simultaneously. Identifying marketplace exchange takes more than proposing that a central plaza was a marketplace. Contextual and distributional evidence are also required. Since these lines of evidence are available from relatively few places, claims about the abundance of marketplaces remain speculative. Maya cities were probably not as commercialized as Tlatelolco/Tenochtitlan or Teotihuacan but it should be noted that such central Mexican behemoths were outliers (Manzanilla 2012: 55). Like Maya settlements, the more numerous, smaller central Mexican cities were also not as commercialized as Tenochtitlan. Maya settlements can be arranged on a continuum from less commercial to more commercial (Garraty 2010: 18; Masson & Freidel 2013: 221). The specific mix of forms of exchange probably varied in relation to settlement size and degree of political centralization. Perhaps the high degree of commercialism at places like Caracol, Tikal, and Chunchucmil was unique to large cities. However, researchers working at smaller sites argue that marketing played an important role in rural economies as well. For example, Scarborough and Valdez (2009) maintain that resource-specialized communities in northwest Belize were economically interdependent and exchanged surpluses with each other in rural markets.

6.3 Currency and the Role of Women in Markets

Combining a discussion of currency and women may seem arbitrary. However, the two most prominent forms of currency in the Maya world – cacao beans and textiles – were both strongly linked to women. Women produced most textiles and cacao has many connections to women. Cacao trees were often owned by women at the time of Spanish contact, cacao trees were personified as female ancestors, and cacao beans were a common dowry paid by the wife's family (Harrison-Buck 2017). Acknowledging the connections between currency and women underscores the point that economic power derives not strictly from the accumulation of material goods, but from the ability to influence social relations of production. Women literally wove money together while marriage negotiations and the regeneration of kinship lines occasioned large transfers of cacao bean currency. The gendered relations of production and exchange of key currencies invite further consideration of women in commerce. Marketplaces were public domains in which Mesoamerican women played extensive roles. In Aztec marketplaces, women worked as both vendors and administrators. Though some women who worked in markets may have been poor (Brumfiel 1991), they could both gain prosperity in the market and, as administrators, control some aspects of its development. In other words, marketplaces appear to be a realm in which women could excel (Blanton 2013) and contest unequal gender ideologies. Ethnohistorical evidence from the Maya area implies strong participation of women not only as buyers and sellers in the marketplace (King 2015b) but also as participants in long-distance trade voyages: Christopher Columbus found women on a seagoing merchant's canoe off the coast of Honduras. The murals in the Calakmul marketplace confirm what ethnohistorical sources suggest; they depict both women and men selling various goods, implying that the marketplace featured as much social diversity as could be seen at Tlatelolco.

Circling back to currencies, money functions in many ways: as a unit of account (a measure of how much something is worth), a medium of exchange (coin, for example, given in return for product), a store of value that can be used as payment (e.g. a pile of cash), and so on. Cacao beans work poorly as a store of value since they degrade after a year. Other candidates for currency in the Maya area that fulfill these three characteristics were present in the Classic period, and were mentioned as currency during the Contact period include textiles, beads (of spondylus and jade), and salt (Freidel et al. 2002). While there is no specific archaeological evidence for the use of beads and salt as currency, Baron (2018) provides clues to when cotton textiles may have been monetized. Based on a lack of standardization of textiles as seen in the seventh-century Calakmul Chiik Nahb murals and clear standardization visible as homogenous piles of textiles in tribute scenes on painted pots from the eighth century, Baron argues that cotton textiles became a plausible unit of account in the eighth century. A rise in the frequency of spindle whorls for spinning cotton thread at Tikal in the Late Classic strengthens the possibility that textiles served as currency.

The notion that a common form of money may have only come online by the late seventh century invites the question of whether earlier markets could get along in the absence of currency. In other words, what about barter, defined as transactions without a medium of exchange? The question of barter is thorny. Economists have imagined that barter was once the norm until its chief inefficiency – waiting around for a "double coincidence of wants" (when a person, for example, who needs obsidian and has extra grinding stones must find that rare someone who needs grinding stones and has extra obsidian) – incentivized the creation of money. While a bit of barter takes place from time to time, anthropologists are unequivocal that barter-based economies as imagined by economists (much less economies that switch from barter to money) have never been documented (Graeber 2011: 29). Proposals about barter in ancient societies of the Americas in fact redefine barter, consciously (Eppich 2020) or unconsciously (Stanish & Coben 2013), as balanced reciprocity.

7 Political Economy

In what ways did centralized authorities shape ancient Maya economies? What aspects of production, distribution, and consumption did they control? Did geopolitical rivalries impact the flow of goods? How often did polity leaders and their subjects interact directly? Earlier understandings promoted a dual-economy model consisting of an exalted sphere involving prestigious goods (exquisite polychrome pottery and stone sculpture) and a mundane sphere involving farming and production of basic goods like stone tools and utilitarian pottery. Undoubtedly, some of the more rural areas of the Maya world featured relatively few interactions between high- and low-status people (Scarborough & Valdez 2009), yet other studies (Masson & Freidel 2012) as well as some of the cases presented in this Element, such as the involvement of both noble and humble households in jade ornament production (see Section 5.1), highlight the growing realms of entanglement among people of various stations in life. The marketplace itself brought together many different sectors of Maya society (McAnany 2010: 267). Furthermore, the supposedly stark distinction that the dual economy model posited between luxury and everyday goods fails to capture the continuum of value that elides the two. For example, greenstone artifacts include rare carved jade pendants but also more widely available serpentine celts and gradiations in between these two poles (Masson & Freidel 2012).

Leaders preoccupied with intra-polity factionalism, inter-polity diplomacy, revenue generation, ritual performance, and other enterprises would not have had the time or resources to organize the redistribution of common goods such as stone tools, pots, baskets, food, lime, clothing, medicine, and so on (Stark & Garraty 2010: 44; Masson & Freidel 2013: 207). Yet leaving this to the market would not have cut the leaders out of the picture. To what extent could leaders have controlled markets? Did markets, as Adam Smith argued in 1776, arise organically, independent of top-down political control, when the number of buyers and sellers grows to a point where convenience demands a marketplace? Or did government regulate markets heavily, as Polanyi thought, or even create them in order to convert tax and tribute into resources needed for armies

(Graeber 2011: 50)? Clearly, leaders had some degree or oversight of markets at the center of Maya cities. Leaders benefitted from sponsoring marketplaces, gaining an outlet for converting staple goods into wealth goods and vice versa, gaining a degree of prestige or symbolic capital as marketplace hosts, and perhaps collecting fees from vendors. Even with oversight, markets can be disorderly. Ethnohisotrical sources note that markets are social as much as economic spaces, full of the kind of spectacle, liminality, and excitement characteristic of large gatherings of strangers (Hutson 2000; Blanton 2013).

A second question regarding political control is how did political competition affect marketplace exchange? Stated differently, to what degree did commerce cross the boundaries of geopolitical rivals? Carol Smith (1976) addressed this issue by contrasting closed market systems ("solar central place") with open market systems ("interlocking"). In a closed system, each polity would have a major market in its capital and producers in the hinterlands were only able to use markets at their capital. In this system, a limited amount of goods crossed polity boundaries. Alternatively, in an open market system, political boundaries do not heavily affect economic boundaries. Smaller markets located in second-ary settlements should flourish, goods could move from a market in one polity to a market in another, and people have choices of which markets to frequent. Maya commerce in the Classic period appears to exhibit aspects of both closed and open systems simultaneously, with variation across space and time and from product to product. For example, archaeologists at Tikal excavated millions of obsidian artifacts, whereas very little obsidian has been recovered from Tikal's arch rival, Calakmul (Volta et al. 2020). Likewise, Calakmul had abundant access to jade, whereas Tikal had less of it until they prevailed over Calakmul at the end of the seventh century. Clouding this picture is the fact that subordin-ate Late Classic allies of Calakmul, such as La Corona and Uxul, had copious amounts of what their overlord lacked – obsidian – while at the same time using pottery very similar to Calakmul's (Volta et al. 2020). Thus, geopolitical networks only partly explain access to goods. Long-distance traders (the *p'olom*) may have slipped across geopolitical fault lines. Reports of markets at smaller Classic period centers like Motul de San José, Buenavista, and Trinidad de Nosotros lead Masson and Freidel (2012: 478, 2013: 220) to argue for interlinked market systems. Sheets (2000) argues that villagers at Cerén in El Salvador had a choice of which markets to use, thus implying an interlinked market system. Tokovinine and Beliaev (2013: 170–2) review contact era ethnohistorical sources from highland Chiapas that indicate volu-minous trade across political boundaries, falling in line with a broader argument about more intensive commercialism in the Postclassic (Sabloff & Rathje 1975).

Outside of the market, royalty collected tribute in the form of jade, quetzal feathers, cacao, spondylus shell, and textiles. Several painted ceramic vases from the Late Classic depict the presentation of tribute and some of these show scribes who may be tallying the amounts of goods collected (McAnany 2010: 284). Warfare often established tributary relations across polities and captives could be ransomed (McAnany 2010: 281). In accord with a well-worn political economy playbook, a portion of this tribute in wealth goods was redistributed to allies and other clients in order to expand and strengthen loyalty and state power. Ringle and colleagues (2020) provide an interesting extension of this principle. In the Puuc hills of Northern Yucatan, archaeologists have found that a very large portion of houses (often above 30 percent) had vaulted stone roofs. Given the specialized skill and high labor cost involved in their construction, vaulted buildings are rare elsewhere, suggesting only very wealthy and/or high-status people occupied them. In the Puuc area, with sometimes a third of the population living in vaulted buildings, such buildings no longer mark high status. Ringle and colleagues argue that lords supported skilled stoneworkers with food collected as tribute, and since palace construction did not provide enough year-round work for their attached builders, the lords had them con-struct clients' houses as an act of largesse and royal patronage. Thus, vaulted roofs may signify not wealth and/or status but cronyism.

The example of attached builders reopens the issue of labor. In Section 5, I argued that the category of attached specialist suffers from the fact that specialists working for a patron often also work for themselves. Yet any tourist who has gazed upon the megalithic Kinich Kak Moo platform at Izamal (measuring 17 m high and an astonishing 4 ha at its base), the Palace of the Governor at Uxmal, or Temple IV at Tikal, recognizes the massive amounts of labor harnessed by ancient kings. The construction of monumental architecture would appear to be a clear index of powerful political economies. We currently do not have much data about labor extraction. Some labor may have been remunerated through redistribution, some might have been corvee (intermittent and unpaid, a version of tribute). In the contact period, slavery provided nobles with a major source of wealth and was therefore a cornerstone of political economies.

The elephant in the room regarding monumental architecture and political economy is that the largest single construction in the Maya world – the platform at Aguada Fenix (Inomata et al. 2020) – was built in the Early Middle Preclassice, prior to sedentism and in the absence of a recognizable political economy. Several other very large constructions were built at other sites with minimal human political hierarchy in the Early and Late Middle Preclassic. The implication is that monumental architecture began in the context of what

Sahlins (Graeber & Sahlins 2017) calls cosmopolitics, in which obligations were to sacred, nonhuman forces. I suspect that monumental construction in later periods always involved some degree of genuinely endorsed cosmopolitical motives, even in the contexts of rulers whose other actions give us license for cynicism regarding motives for extraction of labor.

To the extent that Puuc rulers decided who would live in vaulted houses, this example brings us to the question of sumptuary laws. The Aztecs of Central Mexico enforced regulations about what kinds of dress and ornament pertain to which social positions. Ancient Maya leaders limited the distribution of certain goods (what Freidel & Reilly [2010] call "treasure"). They may also have inspired their followers to consume some of the same items that the leaders themselves flaunted. According to Pyburn (2008),

> elites benefited from making consumption desirable, possible, and safe .... One way elites stimulate markets and consumption is by sponsoring pageants, including sporting events, feasts, public displays, pilgrimages, and various sorts of aesthetic competition ... the elites who sponsor [competitions] and retain the right to pick the winners implicitly verify their right to set standards of excellence and taste and motivate consumer practices to their own advantage.

Close attention to consumption patterns shows that at sites like Tikal, households with more resources tended to consume greater amounts of exotic goods, as if they were following standards of value set by leaders. However, at other sites, households with respectable resources chose not to consume like mini-elites: They pursued different values and likely achieved a quality of life not immediately tied to material possessions (Hutson 2023).

8 Future Directions

I end this Element by highlighting questions and types of research that can pace new progress in our understanding of ancient Maya economies. I cannot put enough stress on the need for more household archaeology. Given that households were the basic units of ancient Maya economies, the only robust route forward is excavation of representative samples of domestic compounds. Let me be clear. A representative sample must contain (at least) dozens of residential compounds encompassing all geographic sectors of a site and the full breadth of wealth levels, with an emphasis on the vast array of non-noble households. This work is not glamorous, but it will advance our knowledge of most of the central topics of this Element: exchange, production, consumption, and inequality.

Regarding exchange, too many studies of commerce focus on a plaza. A plaza might have been a marketplace, but in most cases information from a plaza will be equivocal without an understanding of the distribution of goods across households. Even at Calakmul, whose Chiik Nahb complex already provides very strong evidence for its status as a marketplace, systematic household excavations well beyond the site core would make an extraordinary contribution. Calakmul was the most powerful Classic period metropolis, yet we know little about how its households contributed to the site's strength (did they engage in specialized production?) or benefitted economically from its triumphs (what level of consumption did they enjoy?). Calakmul's political economy is already peculiar, as I describe in Section 7, given that its macro-regional clout did not give it dependable access to obsidian. Getting a fuller picture would crack the nut of its political economy. I don't mean to pick on Calakmul. Household archaeology would benefit any number of sites. Perhaps Chichen Itza is the most egregious example. Masson and Peraza Lope (2014) have provided excellent economic data from Mayapan, the primary Northern Lowland political population center in the Postclassic period. Yet we know next to nothing about household economies from Chichen, Mayapan's immediate political and demographic predecessor and the key site for sorting out the massive changes in the Mesoamerican world system and the transformation of Maya governance during the transition from Classic to Postclassic. Investigations of Chichen's site core show unprecedented access to long-distance goods (Stanton et al. 2023) and a potential market system (Braswell & Glascock 2002) but minimal sampling beyond the core keeps us in the dark about how household economies articulated with long-distance exchange.

Exploration of household economies will likely make an even larger splash when applied to Preclassic Maya societies. This Element focuses primarily on the Classic period because relatively few projects have examined households from the Preclassic period. Archaeologists have succeeded in documenting long-distance trade of exotic artifacts in the Preclassic period and monumental construction boomed at several sites across the Maya world during this time, including Kaminaljuyú, Cerro Maya, Tikal, Yaxuna, Cival, Ceibal, Calakmul, Xocnaceh, and El Mirador. The existence of trade and mechanisms for organizing labor indicate a complex economy. However, without extensive excavations of a representative sample of domestic compounds, we can't say much about patterns of production, distribution, and consumption. Learning about these is important because it can inform us about change over time and the development of the components of the Classic period economies described in this Element.

Systematic testing of domestic compounds at any site for any time period will help discriminate between different forms of intra-site exchange and sort out the relative importance of these forms across space and time. Yet archaeologists will need to interpret household assemblages not just through the lens of exchange but also through the lens of consumption. As opposed to attributing uneven distributions of particular household goods to the shortcomings of a settlement's exchange systems or to a household's lack of purchasing power, it may be more prudent to attribute such uneven distributions to differing household decisions regarding which goods to value (Hutson & Golden 2024).

Household archaeology must be coupled with additional paleoecological work. Lidar has made a robust contribution to production by helping with estimates of the extent of intensive agriculture in the form of terracing and wetland fields. Unexplored areas of wetland fields in southwestern Campeche await paleoecological ground-testing. Now that we have what many of us believe is definitive proof of high Late Classic population densities, pinning down the scale and locations of intensive farming will give us a sharper picture of economic adaptations such as cross-polity trade in bulk goods.

Economic research can also mesh with settlement scaling research. Settlement scaling theory predicts that productivity should rise in larger and more densely settled Maya cities. This is because higher-density settlement affords more contact between residents and this increase in the amount of contacts between people of varied backgrounds permits the flow of ideas and information and the extension of social networks. Yet mere higher density does not necessarily imply more contact, and not all forms of contact increase productivity. What conditions in the Maya area promoted the social mixing that supposedly makes cities economic reactors? Getting at this question requires evaluating the kinds of neighborhoods that existed and the sorts of integrative features (plazas, markets, ceremonies, and pedestrian circulation patterns) found in cities. Does population density correlate with these features? How do they correlate with productivity?

The rise of portable XRF and other archaeometric methods will help trace larger and newer realms of objects from source to producer to consumer. Yet we know little about the organization of the people who moved raw materials and finished goods across the Maya area. Merchants were major power brokers at sites like Cancuen (Demarest et al. 2020) and Chunchucmil, whereas merchants were, frankly, disrespected at the royal courts of other lowland sites. The degree to which long-distance traders, such as the *p'olom* mentioned above, acted as political agents (as among the Aztecs) or independent contractors probably varied from site to site. But we just don't know. Pressing a bit further on the Cancuen/Chunchucmil comparison, leaders at both sites invested heavily in long-distance exchange. Yet Cancuen, in contrast to Chunchucmil, appears not to have had a market. How is it that a rise in mercantile power did not result in across-the-boards prosperity?

Some research questions might eternally resist our efforts. We are unlikely to learn much more about ancient currencies. Likewise, we may never be able to pin down the identity, affiliations, and demography of long-distance traders, from porters to cartel chiefs. The details of human labor extraction, so well-known in other new world contexts such as the Inka of South America, may also elude us perpetually. On the positive side, much of the content of this Element could not have been written thirty years ago. I am eager to see how this Element will be rewritten thirty years in the future.

References

Acabado, S. (2013). Defining Ifugao Social Organization: "House," Field, and Self-Organizing Principles in the Northern Philippines. *Asian Perspectives*, *52*(2), 161–189.

Alston, R. (1998). Trade and the City in Roman Egypt. In H. M. Parkins & C. Smith (Eds.), *Trade, Traders and the Ancient City* (pp. 168–202). London: Routledge.

Andrews, A. P. (1983). *Maya Salt Production and Trade*. Tucson: University of Arizona Press.

Aoyama, K. (1995). Microwear Analysis in the Southeast Maya Lowlands: Two Case Studies at Copan Honduras. *Latin American Antiquity*, *6*(2), 129–144.

Aoyama, K. (2001). Classic Maya State, Urbanism, and Exchange: Chipped Stone Evidence from the Copan Valley and Its Hinterland. *American Anthropologist*, *103*, 346–360.

Ardren, T., Alonso Olvera, A., & Manahan, T. K. (2016). The Artisans of Terminal Classic Xuenkal, Yucatan, Mexico: Gender and Craft during a Time of Economic Change. In S. E. Kelly & T. Ardren (Eds.), *Gendered Labor in Specialized Economies: Archaeological Perspectives on Female and Male Work* (pp. 91–116). Boulder: University Press of Colorado.

Ashmore, W., & Wilk, R. (1988). Household and Community in the Mesoamerican Past. In R. Wilk & W. Ashmore (Eds.), *Household and Community in the Mesoamerican Past* (pp. 1–27). Albuquerque: University of New Mexico Press.

Ashmore, W., & Willey, G. R. (1981). A Historical Introduction to the Study of Lowland Maya Settlement Patterns. In W. Ashmore (Ed.), *Lowland Maya Settlement Patterns* (pp. 3–18). Albuquerque: University of New Mexico Press.

Astor-Aguilera, M. A. (2010). *The Maya World of Communicating Objects: Quadripartite Crosses, Trees, and Stones*. Albuquerque: University of New Mexico Press.

Baron, J. P. (2018). Ancient Monetization: The Case of Classic Maya Textiles. *Journal of Anthropological Archaeology*, *49*, 100–113.

Batun Alpuche, A. I., McAnany, P., & Dedrick, M. (2020). Yucatec Land and Labor before and after the Spanish Incursions. In M. Masson, D. A. Freidel & A. A. Demarest (Eds.), *The Real Business of Ancient Maya Economies: From Farmers' Fields to Rulers' Realms* (pp. 210–224). Gainesville: University Press of Florida.

Beach, T., Luzzadder-Beach, S., Krause, S., Guderjan, T., Jr., F. V., Fernandez-Diaz, J. C., . . . Doyle, C. (2019). Ancient Maya Wetland Fields Revealed under

Tropical Forest Canopy from Laser Scanning and Multiproxy Evidence. *Proceedings of the National Academy of Sciences, 116*(43), 21469–21477.

Becker, M. (2003). A Classic-Period Barrio Producing Fine Quality Ceramics at Tikal Guatemala. *Ancient Mesoamerica, 14*, 95–112.

Berdan, F. F. (1983). The Reconstruction of Ancient Economies: Perspectives from Archaeology and Ethnohistory. In S. Ortiz (Ed.), *Economic Anthropology: Topics and Theories, Monograph in Economic Anthropology No. 1* (pp. 83–95). Lanham, MD: University Press of America.

Bettencourt, L. M. A., & West, G. (2010). A Unified Theory of Urban Living. *Nature, 467*, 912–913.

Blanton, R. E. (1985). A Comparison of Early Market Systems. In S. Plattner (Ed.), *Markets and Marketing* (pp. 399–416). Lanham, MD: University Press of America.

Blanton, R. E. (2013). Cooperation and the Moral Economy of the Marketplace. In K. G. Hirth & J. Pillsbury (Eds.), *Merchants, Markets and Exchange in the Pre-Colombian World* (pp. 23–48). Washington, DC: Dumbarton Oaks Research Library and Collections.

Blanton, R. E., & Fargher, L. F. (2010). Evaluating Causal Factors in Market Development in Premodern States: A Comparative Study, with Critical Comments on the History of Ideas about Markets. In C. P. Garraty & B. L. Stark (Eds.), *Archaeological Approaches to Market Exchange in Ancient Societies* (pp. 207–227). Boulder: University Press of Colorado.

Braswell, G. E., & Glascock, M. D. (2002). The Emergence of Market Economies in the Ancient Maya World: Obsidian Exchange in Terminal Classic Yucatan, Mexico. In M. D. Glascock (Ed.), *Geochemical Evidence for Long-Distance Exchange* (pp. 308–334). Westport, CT: Bergin and Garvey.

Brown, L. A., & Emery, K. F. (2008). Negotiations with the Animate Forest: Hunting Shrines in the Guatemalan Highlands. *Journal of Archaeological Method and Theory, 15*(4), 300–337.

Brumfiel, E. M. (1980). Specialization, Market Exchange and the Aztec State: A View from Huexotla. *Current Anthropology, 21*(4), 459–478.

Brumfiel, E. M. (1991). Weaving and Cooking: Women's Production in Aztec Mexico. In J. M. Gero, & M. Conkey (Eds.), *Engendering Archaeology: Women in Prehistory* (pp. 224–251). Oxford: Blackwell.

Brumfiel, E. M., & Earle, T. (1987). Specialization, Exchange and Complex Societies: An Introduction. In E. Brumfiel, & Timothy Earle (Eds.), *Specialization Exchange and Complex Societies* (pp. 1–9). Cambridge: Cambridge University Press.

Callaghan, M. G. (2016). Observations on Invisible Producers: Engendering Pre-Columbian Maya Ceramic Production. In S. E. Kelly & T. Ardren (Eds.),

Gendered Labor in Specialized Economies: Archaeological Perspectives on Female and Male Work (pp. 267–300). Boulder: University Press of Colorado.

Callaghan, M. G., & Kovacevich, B. A. (2020). The Complexity of Ancient Maya Craft Production. In S. R. Hutson & T. Ardren (Eds.), *The Maya World* (pp. 540–558). New York: Routledge.

Canuto, M. A., Estrada-Belli, F., Garrison, T. G. et al. (2018). Ancient Lowland Maya Complexity as Revealed by Airborne Laser Scanning of Northern Guatemala. *Science, 361*(1355), 1–17.

Carrasco Vargas, R., Vásquez López, V. A., & Martin, S. (2009). Daily Life of the Ancient Maya Recorded in Murals. *Proceedings of the National Academy of Science, 106*(46), 19245–19249.

Chase, A. F., & Chase, D. Z. (1998). Scale and Intensity in Classic Period Maya Agriculture: Terracing and Settlement at the "Garden City" of Caracol, Belize. *Culture and Agriculture, 20*, 60–77.

Chase, A. F., Chase, D. Z., Fisher, C. T., Leisz, S. J., & Weishampel, J. F. (2012). Geospatial Revolution and Remote Sensing LiDAR in Mesoamerican Archaeology. *Proceedings of the National Academy of Sciences, 109*(32), 12916–12921.

Chase, A. F., Chase, D. Z., Terry, R. E., Horlacher, J. M., & Chase, A. S. Z. (2015). Markets among the Ancient Maya: The Case of Caracol, Belize. In E. M. King (Ed.), *Ancient Maya Marketplaces: The Archaeology of Transient Space* (pp. 226–250). Tucson: University of Arizona Press.

Chase, A. S. Z., & Weishampel, J. F. (2016). Using Lidar and GIS to Investigate Water and Soil Management in the Agricultural Terracing at Caracol, Belize. *Advances in Archaeological Practice, 4*(3), 357–370.

Clark, J. E. (1989). Obsidian: The Primary Mesoamerican Sources. In M. Gaxiola & J. E. Clark (Eds.), *La obsidiana en Mesoamerica* (pp. 299–319). Mexico: Instituto Nacional de Antropologia e Historia.

Clark, J. E., & Houston, S. D. (1998). Craft Specialization, Gender, and Personhood among the Post-conquest Maya of Yucatan, Mexico. In C. L. Costin, & Rita P. Wright. (Eds.), *Craft and Social Identity* (Vol. 8) (pp.31–46). Arlington, VA: American Anthropological Association.

Coe, M. D., & Houston, S. D. (2022). *The Maya, 10th edition*. New York: Thames & Hudson.

Coggins, C. C. (1975). *Painting and Drawing Styles at Tikal: An Historical and Iconographic Reconstruction*. Cambridge, MA: Harvard University Press.

Costin, C. L. (1991). Craft Specialization: Issues in Defining, Documenting, and Explaining the Organization of Production. In M. B. Schiffer (Ed.),

Archaeological Method and Theory (Vol. 3, pp. 1–56). Tucson: University of Arizona Press.

Costin, C. L. (2001). Craft Production Systems. In G. M. Feinman & T. D. Price (Eds.), *Archaeology at the Millennium: A Sourcebook* (pp. 273–328). New York: Kluwer.

Dahlin, B. H., Ardren, T., Hixson, D., & Andrews, A. P. (2017). Perishable Resources Produced for Exchange in the Chunchucmil Economic Region. In S. R. Hutson (Ed.), *Ancient Maya Commerce: Multidisciplinary Research at Chunchucmil* (pp. 221–240). Boulder: University Press of Colorado.

Dahlin, B. H., Bair, D. A., Beach, T., Moriarty, M., & Terry, R. (2010). The Dirt on Food: Ancient Feasts and Markets among the Lowland Maya. In J. E. Staller & M. Carrasco (Eds.), *Pre-Columbian Foodways: Interdisciplinary Approaches to Food, Culture, and Markets in Ancient Mesoamerica* (pp. 191–232). New York: Springer.

Dahlin, B. H., Jensen, C. T., Terry, R. E., Wright, D. R., & Beach, T. (2007). In Search of an Ancient Maya Market. *Latin American Antiquity, 18*(4), 363–384.

Deal, M. (1998). *Pottery Ethnoarchaeology in the Central Maya Highlands.* Salt Lake: University of Utah Press.

Demarest, A. A., Victor, B., Andrieu, C., & Torres, P. (2020). A New Direction in the Study of Ancient Maya Economics: Language, Logic, and Models from Strategic Management Studies. In M. Masson & A. A. Demarest (Eds.), *The Real Business of Ancient Maya Economics: From Farmers' Fields to Rulers' Realms* (pp. 28–54). Gainesville: University Press of Florida.

Dietler, M., & Hayden, B. (Eds.). (2001). *Feasts: Archaeological and Ethnographic Perspectives on Food, Politics, and Power.* Washington, DC: Smithsonian Institution Press.

Dunning, N. P., Beach, T., & Luzzadder-Beach, S. (2020). Ancient Maya Agriculture. In S. R. Hutson & T. Ardren (Eds.), *The Maya World* (pp. 501–518). NewYork: Routledge.

Earle, T. K. (1977). A Reappraisal of Redistribution: Complex Hawaiian Chiefdoms. In T. K. Earle & J. E. Ericson (Eds.), *Exchange Systems in Prehistory* (pp. 213–229). New York: Academic Press.

Eppich, K. (2020). Commerce, Redistribution, Autarky, and Barter: The Multi-tiered Urban Economy of El Perú-Waka. In M. Masson, D. Freidel, & A. Demarest (Eds.), *The Real Business of Ancient Maya Economies: From Farmers' Field to Rulers' Realms* (pp. 149–171). Gainesville: University Press of Florida.

Eppich, K., & Freidel, D. A. (2015). Markets and Marketing in the Classic Maya Lowlands: A Case Study from El Perú-Waka'. In E. M. King (Ed.), *Ancient*

Maya Marketplaces: The Archaeology of Transient Space (pp. 195–225). Tucson: University of Arizona Press.

Farriss, N. M. (1984). *Maya Society Under Colonial Rule: The Collective Enterprise of Survival*. Princeton, NJ: Princeton University Press.

Fedick, S. (Ed.). (1996). *The Managed Mosaic: Ancient Maya Agriculture and Resource Use*. Salt Lake City: University of Utah Press.

Fischer, E. (1999). Cultural Logic and Maya Identity: Rethinking Constructivism and Essentialism. *Current Anthropology, 40*(4), 473–499.

Folan, W., Fletcher, L., May Hau, J., & Florey Folan, L. (2001). *Las ruinas de Calakmul, Campeche, México: un lugar central y su paisaje cultural*. Campeche: Universidad Autonoma de Campeche.

Ford, A. (2020). The Maya Forest: A Domesticated Landscape. In S. R. Hutson & T. Ardren (Eds.), *The Maya World* (pp. 519–539). NewYork: Routledge.

Freidel, D. A. (1981). The Political Economies of Residential Dispersion among the Lowland Maya. In W. Ashmore (Ed.), *Lowland Maya Settlement Patterns* (pp. 371–382). Albuquerque: University of New Mexico Press.

Freidel, D. A., Reese-Taylor, K., & Mora-Marin, D. (2002). The Origins of Maya Civilization: The Old Shell Game, Commodity, Treasure and Kingship. In M. A. Masson & D. A. Freidel (Eds.), *Ancient Maya Political Economies* (pp. 41–86). Walnut Creek, CA: Altamira.

Freidel, D. A., & Reilly III, F. K. (2010). The Flesh of the God: Cosmology, Food, and the Origins of Political Power in Ancient Southeastern Mesoamerica. In J. E. Staller & M. D. Carrasco (Eds.), *Pre-Columbian Foodways Interdisciplinary Approaches to Food, Culture, and Markets in Ancient Mesoamerica* (pp. 635–680). Springer-Verlag: New York.

Freidel, D. A., & Shaw, J. M. (2000). The Lowland Maya Civilization: Historical Consciousness and Environment. In R. J. McIntosh, J. A. Tainter & S. K. McIntosh (Eds.), *The Way the Wind Blows: Climate, History, and Human Action* (pp. 271–300). New York: Columbia University Press.

Garraty, C. P. (2010). Investigating Market Exchange in Ancient Societies: A Theoretical Review. In C. P. Garraty & B. L. Stark (Eds.), *Archaeological Approaches to Market Exchange in Ancient Societies* (pp. 3–32). Boulder: University Press of Colorado.

Glaeser, E. L. (2011). *Triumph of the City*. New York: Penguin.

Golden, C. W., & Scherer, A. (2013). Territory, Trust, Growth, and Collapse in Classic Period Maya Kingdoms. *Current Anthropology, 54*(4), 397–435.

Gomez-Pompa, A., Allen, M. F., Fedick, S. L., & Jimenez-Osornio, J. J. (Eds.). (2003). *The Lowland Maya Area: Three Millennia at the Human-Wildland Interface*. New York: Haworth Press.

Graeber, D. (2011). *Debt: The First 5000 Years*. New York: Melville House.

Graeber, D., & Sahlins, M. (2017). *On Kings*. Chicago, IL: Hau Books.

Granovetter, M. (1985). Economic Action and Social Structure: The Problem of Embeddedness. *American Journal of Sociology*, *91*, 481–510.

Greene, K. (1986). *The Archaeology of the Roman Economy*. Berkeley: University of California Press.

Halperin, C. T., Bishop, R. L., Spensley, E., & Blackman, M. J. (2009). Late Classic (A.D. 600–900) Maya Market Exchange: Analysis of Figurines from the Motul de San José Region, Guatemala. *Journal of Field Archaeology*, *34*(4), 457–480.

Halperin, C. T., & Foias, A. E. (2012). Motul de San Jose Palace Pottery Production: Reconstructions from Wasters and Debris. In A. E. Foias & K. F. Emery (Eds.), *Motul de San Jose: Politics, History, and Economy in a Classic Maya Polity* (pp. 167–193). Gainesville: University Press of Florida.

Hanks, W. (1990). *Referential Practice: Language and Lived Space Among the Maya*. Chicago: University of Chicago Press.

Harrison-Buck, E. (2012). Architecture as Animate Landscape: Circular Shrines in the Ancient Maya Lowlands. *American Anthropologist*, *114*(1), 64–80.

Harrison-Buck, E. (2017). The Coin of Her Realm: Cacao as Gendered Goods among the Prehispanic and Colonial Maya. In J. P. Mathews & T. H. Guderjan (Eds.), *The Value of Things: Prehistoric to Contemporary Commodities in the Maya Region* (pp. 104–123). Tucson: University of Arizona Press.

Haviland, W. (1988). Musical Hammocks at Tikal: Problems with Reconstructing Household Composition. In R. Wilk, & Wendy Ashmore (Eds.), *Household and Community in the Mesoamerican Past* (pp. 121–134). Albuquerque: University of New Mexico Press.

Hendon, J. A. (1991). Status and Power in Classic Maya Society: An Archaeological Study. *American Anthropologist*, *93*, 894–918.

Hirth, K. G. (1998). The Distributional Approach: A New Way to Identify Marketplace Exchange in the Archaeological Record. *Current Anthropology*, *39*(4), 451–476.

Hirth, K. G. (2009). Craft Production, Household Diversification, and Domestic Economy in Prehispanic Mesoamerica. In K. Hirth (Ed.), *Housework: Craft Production and Domestic Economy in Ancient Mesoamerica* (pp. 13–32). Alexandria, VA: Archeological Papers of the American Anthropological Association No. 19. American Anthropological Association.

Hirth, K. G. (2010). Finding the Mark in the Marketplace: The Organization, Development, and Archaeological Identification of Market Systems. In C. P. Garraty & B. L. Stark (Eds.), *Archaeological Approaches to Market Exchange in Ancient Societies* (pp. 227–247). Boulder: University Press of Colorado.

Hirth, K. G., & Pillsbury, J. (2013). Merchants, Markets and Exchange in the Pre-Columbian World. In K. G. Hirth & J. Pillsbury (Eds.), *Merchants, Markets and Exchange in the Pre-Columbian World* (pp. 1–22). Washington, DC: Dumbarton Oaks Research Library and Collections.

Hodge, M. G., & Minc, L. (1990). The Spatial Patterning of Aztec Ceramics: Implications for Prehispanic Exchange Systems in the Valley of Mexico. *Journal of Field Archaeology, 17*, 415–437.

Hohmann, B., Powis, T. G., & Healy, P. F. (2018). Middle Preclassic Maya Shell Ornament Production: Implications for the Development of Complexity at Pacbitun, Belize. In M. K. Brown & G. J. Bey III (Eds.), *Pathways to Complexity: A View from the Maya Lowlands* (pp. 117–146). Gainesville: University Press of Florida.

Houston, S. D. (2014). *The Life Within: Classic Maya and the Matter of Permanence*. New Haven, CT: Yale University Press.

Hutson, S. R. (2000). Carnival and Contestation in the Aztec Marketplace. *Dialectical Anthropology, 25*, 123–149.

Hutson, S. R. (2010). *Dwelling, Identity and the Maya: Relational Archaeology at Chunchucmil*. Lanham, MD: Altamira.

Hutson, S. R. (2016). *Ancient Urban Maya: Neighborhoods, Inequality and Built Form*. Gainesville: University Press of Florida.

Hutson, S. R. (Ed.). (2017). *Ancient Maya Commerce: Multidisciplinary Research at Chunchucmil*. Boulder: University Pres of Colorado.

Hutson, S. R. (2020). Inequality and Social Groups. In S. R. Hutson & T. Ardren (Eds.), *The Maya World* (pp. 407–423). New York: Routledge.

Hutson, S. R. (2021). Distributional Heuristics in Unlikely Places: Incipient Markets and Hidden Commerce. In E. Paris (Ed.), *Urban Commerce in Ancient Mesoamerica* (Vol. 32, pp. 95–108). Arlington, VA: American Anthropological Association.

Hutson, S. R. (2023). Inequality of What: Multiple Paths to the Good Life. In S. R. Hutson & C. Golden (Eds.), *Realizing Value in Mesoamerica: The Dynamics of Desire and Demand in Ancient Economies* (pp. 425–446). New York: Palgrave McMillan.

Hutson, S. R., & Davies, G. (2015). How Material Culture Acted on the Ancient Maya of Yucatan, Mexico. In L. Overholtzer & C. Robin (Eds.), *The Materiality of Everyday Life* (pp. 10–26). Washington, DC: Archaeological Papers of the American Anthropological Association.

Hutson, S. R., Dunning, N. P., Cook, B. D. et al. (2021a). Ancient Maya Rural Settlement Patterns, Household Cooperation, and Regional Subsistence Interdependency in the Río Bec Area: Contributions from G-LiHT. *Journal of Archaeological Research, 77*(4), 550–579.

Hutson, S. R., & Golden, C. (Eds.). (2023). *Realizing Value in Mesoamerica: The Dynamics of Desire and Demand in Ancient Economies*. New York: Palgrave McMillan.

Hutson, S. R., Hare, T. S., Stanton, T. W. et al. (2021b). A Space of One's Own: Houselot Size Among the Ancient Maya. *Journal of Anthropological Archaeology, 64*, 550–579.

Hutson, S. R., & Stanton, T. W. (2007). Cultural Logic and Practical Reason: The Structure of Discard in Ancient Maya Houselots. *Cambridge Archaeological Journal, 17*(1), 123–144.

Inomata, T. (2001). The Power and Ideology of Artistic Creation. *Current Anthropology, 42*(3), 321–349.

Inomata, T., & Triadan, D. (2000). Craft Production by Classic Maya Elites in Domestic Settings: Data from Rapidly Abandoned Structures at Aguateca, Guatemala. *Mayab, 13*, 57–66.

Inomata, T., Triadan, D., Vázquez López, V. A. et al. (2020). Monumental Architecture at Aguada Fénix and the Rise of Maya civilization. *Nature, 580*, 530–533.

Jones, C. (1996). *Excavations in the East Plaza of Tikal* (Tikal Report No. 16). Philadelphia, PA: The University Museum, University of Pennsylvania.

Jordan, J. M., & Prufer, K. M. (2017). Identifying Domestic Ceramic Production in the Maya Lowlands: A Case Study from Uxbenká, Belize. *Latin American Antiquity, 28*(1), 66–87.

Joyce, R. A. (1993). Women's Work: Images of Production and Reproduction in Prehispanic Southern Central America. *Current Anthropology, 34*(3), 255–274.

Kennett, D. J., Prufer, K. M., Culleton, B. J. et al. (2020). Early Isotopic Evidence for Maize as a Staple Grain in the Americas. *Science Advances, 6* (23), 1–11. https://doi.org/10.1126/sciadv.aba32.

King, E. M. (Ed.). (2015a). *Ancient Maya Marketplaces: The Archaeology of Transient Space*. Tucson: University of Arizona Press.

King, E. M. (2015b). The Ethnohistoric Evidence for Maya Markets. In E. M. King (Ed.), *Ancient Maya Marketplaces: The Archaeology of Transient Space* (pp. 33–67). Tucson: University of Arizona Press.

King, E. M. (2020). Modeling Maya Markets. In M. Masson, D. Freidel & A. Demarest (Eds.), *The Real Business of Ancient Maya Economies: From Farmers' Fields to Rulers' Realms* (pp. 14–27). Gainesville: University Press of Florida.

King, E. M., & Shaw, L. C. (2015). Introduction: Research on Maya Markets. In E. M. King (Ed.), *Ancient Maya Marketplaces: The Archaeology of Transient Space* (pp. 3–32). Tucson: University of Arizona Press.

Kohler, T. A., Smith, M. E., Bogaard, A. et al. (2018). Deep Inequality. In T. A. Kohler & M. E. Smith (Eds.), *Ten Thousand Years of Inequality: The Archaeology of Wealth Differences* (pp. 289–317). Tucson: University of Arizona Press.

Kovacevich, B. (2007). Ritual, Crafting and Agency at the Classic Maya Kingdom of Cancuen. In E. C. Wells & K. L. Davis-Salazar (Eds.), *Mesoamerican Ritual Economy* (pp. 67–119). Boulder: University Press of Colorado.

Kovacevich, B. (2016). Gender, Craft Production and the State: Problems with "Workshops." In S. E. Kelly & T. Ardren (Eds.), *Gendered Labor in specialized Economies: Archaeological Perspectives on Female and Male Work* (pp. 301–338). Boulder: University Press of Colorado.

Kovacevich, B. (2017). The Value of Labor: How the Production Process Added Value to Pre-Columbian Maya Jade. In J. P. Mathews & T. Guderjan (Eds.), *The Value of Things: Prehistoric to Contemporary Commodities in the Maya Region* (pp. 17–29). Tucson: University of Arizona Press.

LeCount, L. (1999). Polychrome Pottery and Political Strategies in Late and Terminal Classic Lowland Maya Society. *Latin American Antiquity, 10*(3), 239–258.

LeCount, L. (2001). Like Water for Chocolate: Feasting and Political Ritual among the Late Classic Maya at Xunantunich, Belize. *American Anthropologist, 103*(4), 935–953.

LeCount, L. J., Walker, C. P., Blitz, J. H., & Nelson, T. C. (2019). Land Tenure Systems at the Ancient Maya Site of Actuncan, Belize. *Latin American Antiquity, 30*(2), 245–265.

Lohse, J. C. (2020). Archaic Maya Matters. In S. R. Hutson & T. Ardren (Eds.), *The Ancient Maya World* (pp. 11–28). New York: Routledge.

Lohse, J. C., & Valdez, F. J. (Eds.). (2004). *Ancient Maya Commoners*. Austin: University of Texas Press.

Lopez Varela, S., McAnany, P. A., & Berry, K. (1999). Ceramics Technology at Late Classic K'axob. *Journal of Field Archaeology, 28*(1/2), 177–191.

Macrae, S., & Iannone, G. (2016). Understanding Ancient Maya Agricultural Terrace Systems through Lidar and Hydrological Mapping. *Advances in Archaeological Practice, 4*(3), 371–392.

Martin, S. (2012). Hieroglyphs from the Painted Pyramid: The Epigraphy of Chiik Nahb Structure Sub 1–4, Calakmul, Mexico. In C. Golden, S. D. Houston & J. Skidmore (Eds.), *Maya Archaeology 2* (pp. 60–80). San Francisco, CA: PreColumbian Mesoweb Press.

Masson, M. A. (2000). *In the Realm of Nachan Kan: Postclassic Maya Archaeology at Laguna de On, Belize*. Boulder: University Press of Colorado.

Masson, M. A. (2020). Conclusion: The Ties that Bind. In M. A. Masson, D. A. Freidel & A. A. Demarest (Eds.), *The Real Business of Ancient Maya Economics: From Farmers' Fields to Rulers' Realms* (pp. 464–487). Gainesville: University Press of Florida.

Masson, M. A., & Freidel, D. A. (2012). An Argument for Classic Era Maya Market Exchange. *Journal of Anthropological Archaeology, 31*, 455–484.

Masson, M. A., & Freidel, D. A. (2013). Wide Open Spaces: A Long View of the Importance of Maya Market Exchange. In K. G. Hirth & J. Pillsbury (Eds.), *Merchants, Markets and Exchange in the Pre-Colombian World* (pp. 201–228). Washington, DC: Dumbarton Oaks Research Library and Collections.

Masson, M. A., Freidel, D. A., & Demarest, A. A. (Eds.). (2020). *The Real Business of Ancient Maya Economies: From Farmers' Fields to Rulers' Realms*. Gainesville: University Press of Florida.

Masson, M. A., & Peraza Lope, C. (Eds.). (2014). *Kukulcan's Realm: Urban Life at Ancient Mayapan*. Boulder: University Press of Colorado.

Manzanilla, L. (2012).Neighborhoods and Elite "Houses" at Teotihuacan, Central Mexico. In M.-C. Arnauld, L. Manzanilla & M. E. Smith (Eds.), *The Neighborhood as a Social and Spatial Unit in Mesoamerican Cities* (pp. 55–73). Tucson: University of Arizona Press.

McAnany, P. A. (1993). The Economics of Social Power and Wealth among Eighth Century Maya Households. In J. A. Sabloff & J. S. Henderson (Eds.), *Lowland Maya Civilization in the Eighth Century AD* (pp. 65–90). Washington, DC: Dumbarton Oaks.

McAnany, P. A. (2010). *Ancestral Maya Economies in Archaeological Perspective*. Cambridge: Cambridge University Press.

McAnany, P. A., Thomas, B. S., Morandi, S., Peterson, P. A., & Harrison, E. (2002). Praise the Ajaw and Pass the Kakaw: Xibun Maya and the Political Economy of Cacao. In M. A. Masson & D. A. Freidel (Eds.), *Ancient Maya Political Economies* (pp. 123–139). Walnut Creek, CA: Alta Mira Press.

Monaghan, J. (2000). Theology and History in the Study of Mesoamerican Religions. In J. Monaghan (Ed.), *Supplement to the Handbook of Middle American Indians Volume 6: Ethnology* (pp. 24–49). Austin: University of Texas Press.

Polanyi, K. (1944). *The Great Transformation: The Economic and Political Origins of Our Time*. New York: Rinehart.

Potter, D. R., & King, E. M. (1995). A Heterarchical Approach to Lowland Maya Socioeconomies. In R. M. Ehrenreich, C. L. Crumley & J. E. Levy (Eds.), *Heterarchy and the Analysis of Complex Societies* (pp. 17–32). Arlington, VA: American Anthropological Association.

Pyburn, K. A. (1998). Smallholders in the Maya Lowlands: Homage to a Garden Variety Ethnographer. *Human Ecology, 26*(2), 267–286.

Pyburn, K. A. (2008). Pomp and Circumstance before Belize: Ancient Maya Commerce and the New River Conurbation. In J. Marcus & J. Sabloff (Eds.), *The Ancient City: Perspectives from the Old and New World* (pp. 247–272). Santa Fe, NM: School of American Research,.

Redfield, R., & Villa Rojas, A. (1962). *Chan Kom: A Maya Village*. Chicago: University of Chicago Press.

Reents-Budet, D. (1994). *Painting the Maya Universe: Royal Ceramics of the Classic Period*. Durham, NC: Duke Univesity Press.

Reents-Budet, D., Bishop, R. L., Taschek, J. T., & Ball, J. W. (2000). Out of the Palace Dumps: Ceramic Production and Use at Buenavista del Cayo, Belize. *Ancient Mesoamerica, 11*(1), 99–121.

Reina, R. E., & Hill, R. M. (1978). *The Traditional Pottery of Guatemala*. Austin: University of Texas Press.

Rice, P. M. (1987). Economic Change in the Lowland Maya Late Classic Period. In E. M. Brumfiel & T. K. Earle (Eds.), *Specialization, Exchange and Complex Societies* (pp. 76–85). Cambridge: Cambridge University Press.

Ringle, W., Gallareta Negrón, T., & Bey III, G. J. (2020). Stone for My House: The Economics of Stoneworking and Elite Housing in the Puuc Hills of Yucatan. In M. Masson, D. Freidel, & A. Demarest (Eds.), *The Real Business of Ancient Maya Economics: From Farmers' Fields to Rulers' Realms* (pp. 98–116). Gainesville: University Press of Florida.

Robin, C. (2006). Gender, Farming and Long-Term Change. *Current Anthropology, 47*(3), 409–433.

Robin, C. (2013). *Everyday Life Matters: Maya Farmers at Chan*. Gainesville: University Press of Florida.

Rochette, E. T. (2014). Out of Control: Rethinking Assumptions About Wealth Goods Production and the Classic Maya. *Ancient Mesoamerica, 25*(1), 165–185.

Roys, R. L. (1943). *The Indian Background of Colonial Yucatan*. Washington, DC: Carnegie Institution of Washington.

Sabloff, J. A., & Rathje, W. (1975). The Rise of a Maya Merchant Class. *Scientific American, 233*, 72–82.

Sanders, W. T. (1977). Environmental Heterogeneity and the Evoluton of Lowland Maya Civilization. In R. E. W. Adams (Ed.), *The Origins of Maya Civilization* (pp. 287–297). Santa Fe, NM: School of American Research.

Sanders, W. T., & Price, B. J. (1968). *Mesoamerica: The Evolution of a Civilization*. New York: Random House.

Sanders, W. T., & Webster, D. L. (1988). The Mesoamerican Urban Tradition. *American Anthropologist*, *90*, 521–546.

Scarborough, V. L., & Grazioso Sierra, L. (2015). The Evolution of an Ancient Waterworks System at Tikal. In D. Lentz, N. P. Dunning & V. L. Scarborough (Eds.), *Tikal: Paleoecology of an Ancient Maya City* (pp. 16–45). New York: Cambridge University Press.

Scarborough, V. L., & Valdez, F. J. (2009). An Alternative Order: The Dualistic Economies of the Ancient Maya. *Latin American Antiquity*, *20*, 207–227.

Schortman, E. M., Urban, P. A., & Ausec, M. (2001). Politics with Style: Identity Formation in Prehispanic Southeastern Mesoamerica. *American Anthropologist*, *103*(2), 312–330.

Shafer, H. J., & Hester, T. R. (1983). Ancient Maya Chert Workshops in Northern Belize, Central America. *American Antiquity*, *48*, 519–543.

Sharer, R. J., & Traxler, L. P. (2006). *The Ancient Maya*. 6th ed. Palo Alto, CA: Stanford University Press.

Shaw, L. C. (2012). The Elusive Maya Marketplace: An Archaeological Consideration of the Evidence. *Journal of Archaeological Research*, *20*(2), 117–155.

Sheets, P. (2000). Provisioning the Ceren Household. *Ancient Mesoamerica*, *11*, 217–230.

Sheets, P. (2020). Service Relationships within the Broader Economy of Ceren, a Young Maya Village. In M. Masson, D. Freidel & A. Demarest (Eds.), *The Real Business of Ancient Maya Economies: From Farmers' Field to Rulers' Realms* (pp. 238–255). Gainesville: University Press of Florida.

Shenk, M. K., Borgerhoff Mulder, M., Beise, J. et al. (2010). Intergenerational Wealth Transmission among Agriculturalists: Foundations of Agrarian Inequality. *Current Anthropology*, *51*(1), 65–83.

Smith, C. A. (1976). Exchange Systems and the Spatial Distribution of Elites: The Organization of Stratification in Agrarian Societies. In C. A. Smith (Ed.), *Regional Analysis, vol. 2* (pp. 309–374). New York: Academic Press.

Smith, M. E. (1987). Household Possessions and Wealth in Agrarian States: Implications for Archaeology. *Journal of Anthropological Archaeology*, *6*(4), 297–335.

Speal, S. (2014). The Evolution of Ancient Maya Exchange Systems: An Etymological Study of Economic Vocabulary in the Mayan Language Family. *Ancient Mesoamerica*, *25*(1), 69–113.

Stanish, C., & Coben, L. S. (2013). Barter Markets in the Pre-Hispanic Andes. In K. G. Hirth & J. Pillsbury (Eds.), *Merchants, Markets and Exchange in the Pre-Columbian World* (pp. 419–434). Washington, DC: Dumbarton Oaks Research Library and Collections.

Stanton, T. W., Taube, K. A., Osorio León, J. F. et al. (2023). Urbanizing Paradise: The Implications of Pervasive Images of Flower World Across Chichen Itza. In D. B. Marken & M. C. Arnauld (Eds.), *The Flexible Maya City: Attraction, Contraction, and Planning in Lowland Urban Dynamics* (pp. 342–354). Boulder: University Press of Colorado.

Stark, B. (2007). Pottery Production and Distribution in the Gulf Lowlands of Mesoamerica. In C. A. Pool & G. J. Bey III (Eds.), *Pottery Economics in Mesoamerica* (pp. 147–183). Tucson: University of Arizona Press.

Stark, B. L., & Garraty, C. P. (2010). Detecting Marketplace Exchange in Archaeology: A Methodological Review. In C. P. Garraty & B. L. Stark (Eds.), *Archaeological Approaches to Market Exchange in Ancient Societies* (pp. 33–58). Boulder: University Press of Colorado.

Storey, G. R. (2006). Introduction: Urban Demography of the Past. In G. R. Storey (Ed.), *Urbanism in the Preindustrial World* (pp. 1–26). Tuscaloosa: University of Alabama Press.

Taschek, J. T., & Ball, J. W. (1989). Lord Smoke Squirrel's Cacao Cup: The Archaeological Context and Socio-Historical Significance of the Buenavista "Jauncy Vase." In J. Kerr (Ed.), *The Maya Vase Book, Volume 3*. New York: Kerr Associates.

Taube, K. (2005). The Symbolism of Jade in Classic Maya Religion. Journal Ancient Mesoamerica, 16(1), 23–50.

Taube, K. A. (2018 [2015]). The Classic Maya Maize God: A Reappraisal. *Studies in Ancient Mesoamerican Art and Architecture: Selected Works by Karl Andreas Taube* (pp. 76–93). San Francisco: Precolumbia Mesoweb Press.

Tax, S. (1941). World View and Social Relations in Guatemala. *American Anthropologist*, *43*, 27–42.

Tedlock, D., translator. (1985). *Popol Vuh: The Definitive Edition of the Mayan Book of the Dawn of Life and the Glories of God and Kings*. New York: Simon & Schuster.

Thompson, A. E., Gary M. Feinman, Keith M. Prufer (2021). Assessing Classic Maya Multi-Scalar Household Inequality in Southern Belize. *PLOS One*, *16*, e0248169.

Tokovinine, A., & Beliaev, D. (2013). People of the Road: Trade and Travelers in Ancient Maya Words and Images. In K. G. Hirth & J. Pillsbury (Eds.), *Merchants, Markets and Exchange in the Pre-Columbian World* (pp. 169–200). Washington, DC: Dumbarton Oaks Research Library and Collections.

Tozzer, A. M. (1941). *Landa's Relacion de las Cosas de Yucatan: A Translation*. Cambridge, MA: Peabody Museum of American Archaeology and Ethnology.

Triadan, D., & Inomata, T. (2020). Maya Economic Organization and Power: A View from Elite Households at Aguateca. In M. Masson, D. Freidel, & A. Demarest (Eds.), *Nuts and Bolts of Ancient Maya Ecoomies* (pp. 296–314). Gainesville: University Press of Florida.

Turner, B. L. I. (1974). Prehistoric Intensive Agriculture in the Mayan Lowlands. *Science, 185,* 118–124.

Volta, B., Gunn, J. D., Florey Folan, L., Folan, w. J., & Braswell, G. E. (2020). The Political Geography of Long-Distance Exchange in the Elevated Interior Region of the Yucatan Peninsula. In M. Masson, D. Freidel, & A. Demarest (Eds.), *The Real Business of Ancient Maya Economies: From Farmers' Fields to Rulers' Realms* (pp. 352–367). Gainesville: University Press of Florida.

Wilk, R. (1983). Little House in the Jungle: The Cause of Variation in House Size among Modern Maya. *Journal of Anthropological Archaeology, 2,* 99–116.

Willey, G., & Bullard, W. J. (1965). Prehispanic Settlement Patterns in the Maya Lowlands. In G. Willey (Ed.), *Archaeology of Southern Mesoamerica, Part 1* (Vol. 2, pp. 360–377). Austin: University of Texas Press.

Woodfill, B. (2020). Large-Scale Production of Basic Commodities at Salinas de los Nueve Cerros, Guatemala: Implications for Ancient Maya Political Economy. In M. Masson, D. Freidel, & A. Demarest (Eds.), *The Real Business of Ancient Maya Economies: From Farmers' Fields to Rulers' Realms* (pp. 172–183). Gainesville: University Press of Florida.

Wyatt, A. R. (2012). Agricultural Practices at Chan: Farming and Political Economy in an Ancietn Maya Community. In C. Robin (Ed.), *Chan: An Ancient Maya Farming Community* (pp. 71–88). Gainesville: Unviersity Press of Florida.

Yaeger, J. (2000). The Social Construction of Communities in the Classic Maya Countryside: Strategies of Affiliation in Western Belize. In M. A. Canuto & J. Yaeger (Eds.), *The Archaeology of Communities: A New World Perspective* (pp. 123–141). London: Routledge.

Cambridge Elements ≡

Ancient and Pre-modern Economies

Kenneth G. Hirth

The Pennsylvania State University

Ken Hirth's research focuses on the development of ranked and state-level societies in the New World. He is interested in political economy and how forms of resource control lead to the development of structural inequalities. Topics of special interest include: exchange systems, craft production, settlement patterns, and preindustrial urbanism. Methodological interests include: lithic technology and use-wear, ceramics, and spatial analysis.

Timothy Earle

Northwestern University

Tim Earle is an economic anthropologist specializing in the archaeological studies of social inequality, leadership, and political economy in early chiefdoms and states. He has conducted field projects in Polynesia, Peru, Argentina, Denmark, and Hungary. Having studied the emergence of social complexity in three world regions, his work is comparative, searching for the causes of alternative pathways to centralized power.

Emily J. Kate

The University of Vienna

Emily Kate is bioarchaeologist with training in radiocarbon dating, isotopic studies, human osteology, and paleodemography. Having worked with projects from Latin America and Europe, her interests include the manner in which paleodietary trends can be used to assess shifts in social and political structure, the affect of migration on societies, and the refinement of regional chronologies through radiocarbon programs.

About the Series

Elements in Ancient and Premodern Economies is committed to critical scholarship on the comparative economies of traditional societies. Volumes either focus on case studies of well documented societies, providing information on domestic and institutional economies, or provide comparative analyses of topical issues related to economic function. Each Element adopts an innovative and interdisciplinary view of culture and economy, offering authoritative discussions of how societies survived and thrived throughout human history.